Listening *in the* Afterlife *of* Data

THOUGHT IN THE ACT
A series edited by Erin Manning and Brian Massumi

Listening *in the* Afterlife *of* Data

—— AESTHETICS, PRAGMATICS, AND INCOMMUNICATION

David Cecchetto

Duke University Press   Durham and London   2022

© 2022 Duke University Press
All rights reserved
Printed in the United States of America on acid-free paper ∞
Cover designed by A. Mattson Gallagher
Text designed by Drew Sisk
Typeset in Portrait Text, Canela Text, and IBM Plex Mono
by Copperline Book Services

Library of Congress Cataloging-in-Publication Data
Names: Cecchetto, David, author.
Title: Listening in the afterlife of data : aesthetics, pragmatics, and incommunication / David Cecchetto.
Other titles: Thought in the act.
Description: Durham : Duke University Press, 2022. | Series: Thought in the act | Includes bibliographical references and index.
Identifiers: LCCN 2021020891 (print)
LCCN 2021020892 (ebook)
ISBN 9781478015291 (hardcover)
ISBN 9781478017912 (paperback)
ISBN 9781478022534 (ebook)
Subjects: LCSH: Technology—Philosophy. | Communication and technology—Philosophy. | Communication and technology—Social aspects. | Sound (Philosophy) | Communication and the arts—Philosophy. | BISAC: SOCIAL SCIENCE / Media Studies | PHILOSOPHY / General
Classification: LCC P96.T42 C433 2022 (print) |
LCC P96.T42 (ebook) | DDC 303.48/33—dc23
LC record available at https://lccn.loc.gov/2021020891
LC ebook record available at https://lccn.loc.gov/2021020892

Cover art: (*Front*) Fathead audio delay. (*Back*) Fathead Doppler effect. Illustrations by Luke Painter.

With love, for:

Marshall, lunatic artist and lovable idiot;

Phannie, curmudgeon scientist and empathic savant;

Katherine, more-than and otherwise beyond compare.

CONTENTS

Acknowledgments ix

Introduction Incommunication 1

1 Networking Sound and Medium Specificity 21

2 Listening and Technicity 44

3 Incomputable and Integral
Incommunications 62

4 Algorithms, Art, and Sonicity 84

5 Listening and Technicity (Once and for All,
Again and Again) 105

Postscript Epidemiological Afterlives 124

Appendix Aural Incommunications Seminar Prompt 131

Notes 135   Bibliography 155   Index 163

ACKNOWLEDGMENTS

Many colleagues, institutions, and friends have contributed to what has become this book. Special thanks to my Occulture comrades Marc Couroux, Ted Hiebert, Eldritch Priest, and Rebekah Sheldon, and more broadly to the robust community of Tuning Speculation folks who inspire me to think well and weirdly. This book is peppered with sentences, phrases, and sometimes paragraphs that I've presented at Tuning Speculation conferences or posted at The Occulture (http://www.theocculture .net), and is animated by that community's care and intelligence.

I was very generously hosted by University of New South Wales Art and Design and am grateful for having had the opportunity to work there with the feedback of brilliant faculty and graduate students. I was astounded by the collegial community at UNSW and am thankful to Caleb Kelly and Anna Munster in particular for their work arranging my visit and for welcoming me so capaciously.

The Society for Literature, Science, and the Arts has been a fecund setting for developing this work, through papers and panels but even more through the informal conversations that texture life and ideas alike. I often reflect on the many scholars—too many to name, both junior and senior—who made me feel welcome there when I was a graduate student and have continued to do so. I wish I could name everyone I've learned from at SLSA, but the list would be too long (and many folks are so astonishingly influential that naming could only feel like name-dropping in any case); I'll try to thank everyone in person!

I'm grateful to the Cultural, Social, and Political Thought program at the University of Victoria (and especially then-director—and itinerant thinker in the best sense—Emile Fromet de Rosnay) for twice inviting me to workshop nascent ideas there. The canny students and faculty in that program gave me much food for thought; thanks, too, to Anita Girvan, who has often helped me turn such food into the right kinds of meals. I especially appreciate Arthur Kroker for hosting a lovely meal in his home that, as is always the case with Arthur, was also a much-enjoyed and appreciated lesson in the wondrous proximity of thinking and living. (I wish Marilouise could have joined us.)

I don't even know how to thank Stephen Ross anymore, as he always knows how to do everything and has often applied that ability to my work and career, despite perhaps never really knowing what it is I'm going on about.

Further thanks, in no particular order, to:

- Erin Manning, Brian Massumi, and Elizabeth Ault for their support of this manuscript throughout the process, and Benjamin Kossak for being such a skillful shepherd. Thanks to Erin, too, for a sparkling conversation that catalyzed a new approach to this book, and for her detailed responses to early excerpts.

- Andrea Davis, who chaired my department at York University while I worked on this book. Not only did Andrea always support my research in the material ways one hopes for from one's chair, but she also taught me important lessons about academic leadership that reminded me that changes big and small are possible.

- Luke Painter, for creating the book's illustrations (during a pandemic, no less).

- Colin Clark, Kelly Egan, Renée Lear, Evan Merz, and Juliana Pivato for correspondence about their artistic practices and sharing documentation.

- Anil Bawa-Cavia for his patience and skill while introducing me, in his role as instructor of an online course, to several key mathematical concepts and thinkers.

- Josh Dittrich and Patrick Nickleson, whose extensive feedback and editorial assistance has been a tremendous benefit to this book. I'm thankful for their patience and diligence, but especially for reading my work so generously.

- The anonymous reviewers, each of whom shared capacious time and intelligence toward making this a tangibly better book. I also appreciate the reviewer who contextualized some misgivings with an earlier draft by noting that they may, partially, be matters of personal taste. I read that as an act of generosity, and one that I've since carried forward in my own reviews of manuscripts. The specific content of the review, too, helped me clarify the aims and stakes of this book.

- M. Beatrice Fazi, whose work has been working on me for the past several years and whom I have had the pleasure of befriending in the process of this book coming to fruition. I so enjoy the play of our exchanges, and I swear it isn't just because Beatrice characterizes me as an iconoclast! Truly, I'm grateful for the purchase our conversations have given me on the thoughts of someone whose work is of the utmost seriousness and importance.

- Katherine Behar, whose brilliant and careful attention to the first pages of what became the introduction of this book convinced me to rewrite the whole thing. Katherine's own work, too, has often nudged my thinking in new directions and to new depths.

- William Brent, for longtime friendship, shared jokes, technical inventiveness, and for bearing with me as I work to understand the specific technical elements of our collaborations (also for coauthoring Conflation [http://idiomconflation.com], with which I remain disproportionately pleased).

- Anna, Jasmine, and Sevina, for sustaining the enrichments of "family" even as the meaning of that term continually changes.

- Marshall and Phannie, my most frequent (literal) bedfellows and interlocutors, whose feline latches have levered more than a few of my intuitions into full-blown thoughts.

Research for this book was generously supported by the Social Sciences and Humanities Research Council of Canada.

INTRODUCTION

Incommunication

*In all likelihood, the only thought that can be made
practical is the thought that is not restricted in
advance by the practice to which it is meant to be
immediately applicable.*

THEODOR ADORNO, *LECTURES ON NEGATIVE DIALECTICS*

How might we listen to computers in their incommunicative profiles? To be sure, this is an obscure
question, but such obscurity may be the hallmark of any
good question. A question that has its answer already built
into its problem is less a question and more a calculation: a
finite procedure for passage from one state to another that
any agent would effect in the exact same way.[1] This distinction between a question and a calculation surfaces in various guises throughout the following pages, usually toward
parsing obscurities that are nested within the seemingly
most obvious relations. Pulling out the threads of these
strange but pragmatic excesses in order to state an obvious
question more obscurely is an important step in thinking
the entire situation with greater nuance and more particularity—even when that nuanced particularity is itself productive of generalities! (Sometimes it is important to note
exactly how things are generally true.) Over the course of

this book, then, three concepts (sound, communication, and data) will be obscured and brought together in the obscurity of a question that would chart their interrelations in particular times, places, and constellations. The book offers answers to its guiding question and does so pragmatically by engaging with (often unusual, but) specific entities and undertakings. I discuss collective experiences of listening with one-thousand-foot-wide heads, for example, as well as strange nonvisual digital audio workstations, intermedially perceptive basketball stars, quasi-suicidal dreams, and playing squash with an eleven-year-old aspiring member of the Canadian national team.

I emphasize the pragmatism of my approach to this question because it works against one of the great inversions of our time: that between abstraction and reality. This inversion is evidenced by the fact that somehow one daily encounters folks who think that business-related disciplines like marketing are part of a real world that theoretically informed arts and humanities disciplines are not; we're in a cultural moment when claiming something like having a "passion for real estate" sounds coherent. Originally a play of thought, the abstractions of classical logic have become habitual in such a way as to today too often seem aprioristic.[2] Clearly, the constitution of the real world needs to be thought more obscurely—or really, to be practiced in its obscurity—in a time when "the hard materiality of the unreal convinces us that we [must continue to protect] nothing but an illusory right to what we do not have."[3] To do so, we have to resist reducing reality to the abstract values it holds in the exchanges of (post)global capitalism, especially because these exchanges are themselves constituted in and as the antisocial interpersonal dynamics of white, patriarchal dominance. However, before this book proposes answers to its guiding question, the remainder of this introductory chapter will focus on offering some purchase on the question itself.

The impossibility of communication is a trope that variously appears in diverse historical and cultural settings. J. D. Peters outlined this brilliantly in his history of the idea of communication, *Speaking into the Air*, noting the historicity of "communication," the varied senses of the term, and the different disciplinary and creative approaches toward it. Put simply, Peters is interested in communication as "one of the characteristic *concepts* of the twentieth century," and as such he tracks its conceptual latches, mutations, and vagrancies; as often as not, these are most perceptible in and as communicative failures.[4]

Peters unfurls a complex narrative throughout the course of *Speaking into the Air* that merits attention in its own right, and that has had a certain well-deserved influence. And yet one of the things that has most stuck with me as the book has aged is a certain kind of formulation—a certain trope—that expresses itself in several places throughout. This trope is that of a reciprocal causality between communications and the perspectives or disciplines from which they are understood as such. For example, discussing the distinctly psychological perspective that humans are "hardwired by the privacy of our experiences to have communication problems [such that] the impossibility of communication between minds may be a fundamental psychological fact," Peters notes in passing that this impossibility may alternately be understood as "the fundamental fact of the field of psychology."[5] We can observe a similar dynamic if we approach communication informatically: by conceptualizing communication in terms of signals that are subject to noise, we describe a situation in which communications are literally hardwired to be noisy by the physical systems in which they are enacted. However, just as the impossibility of intersubjective communication establishes the possibility of psychology as a field, the impossibility of a noiseless transmission is foundational to the field of informatics. The point, which is a resonant theme throughout *Speaking into the Air*, is that part of communication's historicity—that is, part of communication's historical changes in its concepts, practices, and materialities—comes about by virtue of its being always caught up in something that at once exceeds and conditions it.

Of course, this observation of a feedback relation between "whats" and "hows" is by no means unique to the concept of communication: if a person with only a hammer tends to treat everything as a nail, the corollary to this is that additional tools will procure additional hardware. Moreover (as McLuhan knew well), multiplying tools also retunes existing hardware such that a conventional nail might look like an impediment to speedy labor to a person with a pneumatic nail gun. As Patricia Ticineto Clough notes (in a discussion of measurement), "there is a participation of the [observing/ measuring] and the [observed/measured] in which the participation in one another is affective," which is to say, beyond measurement proper.[6] In whatever context one considers it—from quantum physics to manual labor—

Introduction   3

observation is itself at once historical, contingent, and in some sense occultly impactful on that which is being observed.

And yet there is something else worth noting specifically about the communicative profile of this reciprocity. If every communication is a what-how coupling, then "whats" and "hows" are not only entangled in the causal tautologies of feedback, they are also in secondary feedback loops with something that can't be explained because it exceeds communication. This is something that is "artful" in that it "is about how a set of conditions coalesce to favor the opening of a process to its inherent collectivity, to the more-than of its potential."[7] This "aesthetic yield" is also historically affective in that it charts the terrain of a bidirectional relationship between communications and their conditions of appearance.[8] The causal knots themselves—the observation/observer couplings—are enactive: they condition the conditions that condition them. This in turn means that a failure of communication is always also something of an unknowable and paradoxical excess: the impossibility of fully communicating one's psyche, then, is not only the fundamental fact of the field of psychology but also precisely the disclosure of something quasi-psychological that remains outside of psychology. That is, there is something psychologically aesthetic.

To invoke aesthetics in this way is to understand it—following Deleuze—as an investigation into the real conditions of experience that exceed representation. Conceptually, aesthetics is thus intertwined with affect and excess. The terms are not precisely interchangeable, but they are also never entirely extricable from one another: throughout this book I use *aesthetic* to indicate something like a motive, value-laden, inarticulable sensory knowledge that at once grounds and exceeds valuation, and does so according to multiple, not necessarily coherent temporalities. I invoke the term *affect* similarly, but usually in relation to signification rather than value per se, with the term *excess* nominating the performativities that are always immanent to these and other constative claims.

With respect to the "psychologically aesthetic," Erin Manning powerfully parses this concatenation in her work on neurotypicality and neurodiversity, wherein she limns an ecological understanding of perception: perception, for Manning, is always first of an ecology, and only secondarily of subjects and objects.[9] In making this clear, Manning works from the ways that people with autism gradually form the entities of their environment rather than instantaneously engaging in the reductive chunking of neurotypicals. Importantly in the present context, this chunking includes the production of interiority (i.e., the subject). Manning thus demonstrates that the interiority that is constitutive of psychology is not a given, but is rather the result of psychological practices; like all practices, these are never fully determinate, always in progress, and always productive of and in conjunction with a more-than-themselves.

Put differently—and to move toward introducing incommunication, a key concept through which this book (in)coheres[10]—the impossibility of communication is always enacted through actual miscommunications that are themselves always also something else, something that can never quite be fully articulated. This is the lesson of Peters's trope: communication isn't just another observation/observer conundrum but also constitutes the conundrum itself in and as the actualization of a process that (like every enaction) is productive of excesses that can never themselves quite be observed. Aligning with Whitehead's well-known concept of "nonsensuous perception," we might say that there is a force of observation that is at work before it actualizes as a process and that persists as a strange excess to that which is observed. That is, there is something parasitic in communication that makes it a system that "works because it does not work."[11] Echoing Manning—herself echoing Moten and Harney—there is a fugitivity at the heart of communication: in communication there is "the quality of a reorientation moved by a spark that connects to an intensity already moving transversally," such that the inevitable mis(s)es of communications create openings for socialities to travel "in directions as yet in germ."[12] Put simply, the impossibility of communication itself—of pure communication—is enacted through actual, material, miscommunications.

I will ultimately argue that this enaction is indicative of (in)communication being first social, rather than indicating something that is secondary to autonomous communicants: as Michel Serres famously argues, the noise in a communicative relation comes before the establishment of a connection between sender and recipient.[13] But it bears noting first that a resonant point to the one I've been making has been argued through an emphasis on excommunication in the book of that name by Galloway, Thacker, and Wark. Emphasizing the fact that "there are certain kinds of messages that state *there will be no more messages*," the authors insist that there is thus a correlative excommunication for every communication, which is to say that "every communication harbors the dim awareness of an excommunication

Introduction   5

that is prior to it, that conditions it and makes it all the more natural."[14] The point, in the context that I am building presently, is that "excommunication is itself communicated": "at the center of excommunication is a paradoxical anti-message, a message that cannot be enunciated [. . . and] that has already been enunciated, asserted, and distributed."[15]

As I am mobilizing it here, incommunication aligns with the assertions proffered by excommunication, as well as with Serres's more widely known argument that (as Marie Thompson puts it) "noise does not simply destroy but constitutes the relation."[16] However, incommunication gives greater emphasis to the role that an appearance of communication plays in latching otherwise incoherent relations to one another. There is (always) something aesthetic in the mix, and it is precisely the excessive relationality of this register that produces the relata that will themselves appear to have produced relations. Incommunication thus works in the future anterior, naming the bundle of materials, concepts, and phenomena that will have been the enaction of communication through miscommunications. In this sense, it is the (non)experience upon which the concepts of aesthetics, affect, and excess converge. Indeed, in this perspective, "miscommunication" is something of a misnomer, since communication is always in some important sense incommunicable.

Put differently, incommunication (in)coheres both transitively and intransitively—it brings specific things together into a specific constellation of relations (i.e., it is transitive), while also naming a process of ongoing, open-ended enaction (intransitive). In this, incommunication highlights the paradoxical sense in which it is not only the case that there is a continuum connecting total, partial, and nonexistent communications, but also that these are each qualitatively distinct: there is something of a partial communication that can't be described in the terms of that communication, because the part is not just a part of something but also its own thing altogether. If both are true, however, they are not equally so because the qualitative distinctions condition the quantitative ones in a way that does not invert. That is, incommunication enunciates the (paradoxical, contingent, relational, and actual) primacy of qualia and asserts the sense in which the relationship between full and nonexistent communication is a nondialectical one. A miscommunication thought incommunicatively is not a partial communication—that is, a part that has been extracted from a whole—but rather its own kind of thing with its own particular affordances: it's not that we've communicated less, but that we've communicated something different. To fail to understand this is to risk erasing precisely what makes a particular communication particular, which is to say, what makes it an incommunication.

And so, if the impossibility of communication appears and reappears throughout a wide range of philosophical, artistic, and cultural histories, it is worth keeping in mind that it does indeed appear. There is something entirely singular about each instance: incommunications are the singularities of every failed communication, and they each have specific textures; they have moments, contexts, trajectories, promiscuities, densities, roughnesses, speeds, buoyancies, frequencies, amplitudes, and so forth. Listening incommunicatively, we are reminded that worlds don't somehow stop worlding during their failures to communicate, even if worlding itself is in some sense the primal act of communication.

At times, I've been tempted to parse this as a problem of attention, thinking that incommunications are clearly perceptible if one simply attends to them closely enough. Indeed, this has been the gambit of a certain history of art wherein to understand art in its historical dimension is to put aside attempts to define art categorically in favor of embracing the ways that aesthetic practices work in tandem with other protean historical processes to articulate moments simultaneously in their absolute particularity and in their contributions to the reproduction of cultures. In the context of completed global capitalism, for example, one such art historical trajectory can be plotted by attending to that in an artwork which unveils something inexchangeable at the heart of an exchange. Ironically, the tropes of this are most familiar in artists' claims that the work of their work is to defamiliarize: such a claim is supported by the contrasting beliefs that experience can be drawn out in its particularity by being made unfamiliar and that experience is always experienced under the threat of departicularization (especially through the various alienating forces that contour contemporary life for the globally privileged).[17]

Even though I'm sympathetic to such a perspective, my sense today is that one is not required to pay particularly close attention in order to perceive incommunications. Instead, they are regularly perceptible in daily life. To feel frustrated—as a very simple example—by the inefficacy of speaking to one's local political representative is to feel a specific impossibility of communication: one has the feeling—which is to say, one knows

Introduction   7

because one feels, and one feels because one knows—that the communicative situation of political representation entirely precludes not only anything like a "matching of minds" but also even anything more pragmatic like "the cultivation of fruitful activity in an evolving community," which is how John Dewey, William James, and Charles Sanders Peirce understood communication.[18] Instead, one feels the qualitative discontinuity between the democratic-informatic myth of being part of a voting populace (which would, in principle, give one a partial say in things) and the lived reality of political disenfranchisement that comes with trying to introduce anything political that is not already accounted for in the mix. Again, particular attention is not really required. One feels this; one knows this. Who really expects the theater of "unprecedented access" to politicians via social media to yield a performance that hasn't been scripted in advance?[19]

So if the impossibility of communication abounds once and for all, it also does so again and again: once and for all in the invariance of the impossibility, but again and again in the particularities of this invariance. Incommunication names this paradox that constitutes communication itself, namely, the fact that communication is a process that is at once impossible and unavoidable, locatable and excessive. Specifically, incommunication names this paradox in its performative dimension, because incommunications come about in the strange singularities of iterability and are constituted always in excess of themselves.

In our present moment (if such a thing can be said to exist) I would venture that the privileged form of incommunication is that of computational data. As Alexander Galloway perversely paraphrases Stuart Hall, "the digital is both the site and the stake in any contemporary struggle."[20] A computational perspective hallucinates an idea of information as something that would remain unchanged as it moves between contexts, such that data can be raw, pure, and fundamentally nonrelational.[21] This is a paradigm no doubt inherited from the interpersonal exchanges of white, patriarchal capitalism, where exchanges fail to cultivate collectivities because they are understood to flow from and return to the presupposed interiority of the individual. However, a computational perspective substitutes data—as discrete bits of information—for the individual in this economy, resulting in what Steven Connor calls an exopistemological perspective: an economy of computational exchange yields knowledge without a knower.[22] As Clough

8   Introduction

explains (via Latour), "with massive amounts of data and the technologies to parse them, access to data about the individual or the collective is always the same: they are [indistinguishable because they are] both nodes of a network."[23]

Incommunicative egresses are particularly palpable when the heterogeneous and incommunicative textures of reality are flattened in this way. Communication might well be—among other things—"the interactive computation of a reality,"[24] but the recursive nature of the relation between individuals and collectives guarantees that any formalist description of either will miss something vital. From an incommunicative perspective, the crucial thing to note about this paradigm of acontextual informatic exchangeability is that it continues to circulate its postcapitalist fever dreams of universal exchange independent of anyone's belief in its communicative disguise. This paradigm can persist even in the absence of understanding or belief per se. For example, nobody knows what a "97 percent match" in the context of a dating app really means—and no reasonable person would take that ranking as indicating that a successful coupling is a foregone conclusion— but the number has a certain allure nonetheless.[25] Likewise, R. Joshua Scannell notes that most individual members of the New York Police Department don't believe in the accuracy of crime-tracking systems and predictive policing data, but act on them regardless.[26] Similarly, we know (from copious studies and statistics) that the lived realities of democratic political processes mean that the two-stage reduction of (first) collectives to individuals and (second) individuals to votes—that is, data points—can never be a fair, level, and robust process for cultivating collective political discourse, but the process is recognized regardless.[27] Like recent studies suggesting that placebos work even when one knows one is being given a sugar pill, consciously knowing that data is a trick doesn't seem to curtail its impact. This is the sense, then, that we are living in the afterlife of data: we are living in a time when data persists as an impactful element in the absence of any material existence.[28]

Because something *is* happening in these exchanges. As Sun-Ha Hong remarks, "what is being sold to us is not what data knows or can do, but what [data] allows us to do in its name."[29] Racist, homophobic, ableist, patriarchal hegemony is actively sustained both through the alibi of data and through the absence of belief in it. The former dissimulates the weight of historical prejudice that is borne in the present through inherited wealth,

Introduction   9

values, and space: the purported neutrality of data underwrites the neoliberal belief in individual agency. The latter—the lack of belief in data—is equally and simultaneously forceful, though, because it provides a plausible deniability against commentary that would deploy the erroneous results of such systems as evidence against the broader neoliberal paradigm of exchangeability. For example, if one were to note the racially disproportionate outcomes of data-driven approaches to policing and, from this, argue that policing itself should be acknowledged as racially biased, the unconvincingness of data offers a built-in response for police to blame the (data-based) implementation of their values rather than the values themselves.[30] Likewise in elections where a fascist's victory is explained as a failure to get a specific demographic's vote out (e.g., the Black or youth vote). Again, it is the appearance of data that sustains both sides of this universal (in)exchangeability such that failed technologies can persistently and repeatedly fail, rather than simply disappearing.[31]

M. Beatrice Fazi—whose agenda-setting work features prominently in the third chapter of this book—connects this understanding of computation as universal exchange to Leibniz's concept of a universal conceptual language that could unambiguously represent all that can be thought and expressed, and that could be acted upon according to a general mathematical science. As Fazi demonstrates, it is "impossible to ignore the influence that [this] dream of universal symbolic calculation has exerted upon the development of contemporary computing" because it crafts "a generalization of the rules of thought itself" that amounts to "an attempt to construct . . . a *machine of thought*."[32] Specifically, Leibniz's perspective gives thinking "an inferential, normative, and procedural form" that is completed in Turing's algorithmic method wherein reasoning becomes axiomatic. Reasoning—in Turing's thought and the computers that come from its legacy—is "fully automated insofar as it needs nothing but itself in order to prove its validity."[33]

Crucially, for Fazi, Leibniz's proposed "machine of thought" and Turing's treatment of thought "as if its behaviour was already similar to that of a machine" work together to suture the notion of calculative validity to generality: "if calculation is valid reasoning . . . , and if valid reasoning always aims to be universal . . . , then a valid calculative method is one that tries to be as general as possible."[34] That is, "the automation of thought thrives on this procedural determinism of rules of inference: it is its com-

10   Introduction

plete determination that makes a machine (of thought, as of anything else) a machine."[35] Simply put, the computational understanding of thought is "predicated upon the assumption that both proof and function can be placed outside of space and time, and outside of context and content."[36] To be blunt: thought is conceived as data, and data is thought as soul.

Of course, there are ample criticisms of this understanding of thought, which inevitably involves abstracting from the spatiotemporal and affective dynamics that are immanent to lived experience. As Fazi concisely summarizes, such processes "can only be reduced to their logical representation by way of the approximation and generalization of those dynamics," which is to say, by robbing them of the dynamism that defines them.[37] And yet it is worth keeping in mind just how deeply naturalized this perspective has become. While it is easy enough to find instances where such deterministic thinking is refused in the name of embodied processes, the logic of generalization nonetheless remains ubiquitous: it is easy enough to say that Facebook interactions, for example, fail to cultivate the level of intimacy that face-to-face conversation affords, but the reasons for this—interindividual affective exchange, shared contextual cues, scents, sounds, touches, and so on—remain generally true rather than singularly so. After all, how could the actual and specific intimacy of a particular interaction be robbed by Facebook if the specific interaction only ever took place on Facebook in the first place? If we feel like we can feel a loss that never actually happens, this suggests that we have given up something of the openness to other possibilities that would have made it special in the first place. In this way, the sense of incompleteness that comes with such interactions further entrenches a formalized, schematic understanding of communication.

The point is, computational communication—the offspring of white, colonial, patriarchal capitalist exchange, adapted for postmaterial consumer culture—crafts a particular topological invariant between humans and machines.[38] Recent geopolitical events demonstrate that "the symbolic order is alive and well, whether it be in the command of the sovereign or the infrastructure of the machine. The digital is the site of contemporary power. The digital is where capital exploits labor. The digital organizes technologies, bodies, and societies."[39] Data is a master schema of the social, and this is only more the case in the era of its afterlife, when it is unfettered by the constraints of actuality. It has become a cliché to note

Introduction 11

the wild abandon with which the term *algorithm* is thrown around, but it is less noted that this irresponsible ubiquity nonetheless actually makes algorithmic thinking more impactful: particular instances might be criticized, but such criticism both reinforces the legitimacy of proper uses of the term and circulates that quality of algorithmic legitimacy as something worth defending.

This is the context in which I offer the neologism *dataphasia*, naming not just that which data cannot speak (which may in fact be unnameable) but also the fact that in important senses computational communication is expressive of the specific ways in which data cannot speak at all because it is at once tied to the fixity of a presumed subject and indistinguishable from networking.[40] This neologism leverages something of a perverse understanding of aphasia wherein it is rethought less as a communicative incapacity and more as an enunciative-receptive situation.[41] That is, this gambit takes the position that an aphasic (non)utterance communicates plenty, so if interlocutors are frustrated it is because the communicational collectivity is incapable of being receptive to that which is communicated that doesn't originate in—and flow directly from—conscious thought. The nonevent of aphasic communication conveys oodles and does so according to the terms that are in play, but in a way that can't be traced to an origin or will. Speech in this way evinces an originary technicity that means it is always under the threat of being wrested from the idealism of conscious thought and self-possessed intention, so that aphasia is in fact the first condition of speech. Analogously to the way that noise comes first for Serres, aphasia enunciates the relation that it seems to impede.

Likewise, in a culture of completed dataphasia there is no shortage of datic (in)communications, but this is the case because the purported content of these—the bits and bytes one hears so much about—are more the effects of social forms (or quasi-consensual hallucinations, if you like) than the agents that they are regularly imagined to be. As Jodi Dean argues, today "values heralded as central to democracy take material form in networked communications technologies," but in doing so, any particular contribution "need not be understood; it need only be repeated, reproduced, forwarded."[42] Since, as Dean concludes, this means that "circulation is the context," the situation is fully dataphasic: the circulation of (in)communications develops an economy that speaks only its own circulation rather

12   Introduction

than particular messages, and this circulation (by the same logic) does not exist except as an aesthetics of computational incommunication. Messages circulate spectrally, evincing and texturing their own nonexistence.

If the computational alibi persists in the face of its having been so thoroughly critiqued, a tack other than critique is called for: "uncut devotion to the critique of this illusion [of politics] makes us delusional."[43] Rather than assuming the Sisyphean task of critiquing communication directly, the gambit of this book is that we might begin by simply listening to these siren songs of smooth computational space. Such a listening would be undertaken not so much in order to show (yet again) the impossibility of communication, but rather to hear what is disclosed in the specifics of the alibi itself, by its appearances.

There are reasons aplenty for adopting listening as a method. Insofar as "resonance"—a key acoustic concept—describes the "patterned intensity of a flow, expressed as a rate or a frequency ratio,"[44] it seems naturally suited to the relational and distributed understanding of agency that incommunication develops, especially in its computational appearance. To listen in this environment is less to craft a stable subject/object relation and more to adopt a posture that acknowledges one's entanglement in ongoing processes of attunement and differentiation. Listening is in this sense not tied to literal sound per se, but is instead a material-semiotic sociotechnical practice that engages the world in its acoustic registers.

And yet, if listening seems like a natural ally for the afterlife of data, that should equally give us pause. In terrible times, anything easy is also suspect. As Robin James has convincingly demonstrated (building on Foucault's concept of the episteme), we live in something of a "sonic episteme," in which "acoustically resonant sound is the 'rule' [that] otherwise divergent practices use 'to define the objects proper to their own study, to form their concepts, to build their theories.'"[45] Moreover, "this rule is the qualitative version of the quantitative rules neoliberal market logics and biopolitical statistics use to organize society."[46] In this way, "the sonic episteme misrepresents sociohistorically specific concepts of sound" as though they were natural, and then "uses sound's purported difference from vision to mark its departure from what it deems the West's ocular- and text-centric status quo."[47] This episteme remakes and renaturalizes the white supremacist political baggage inherited from Western modernity "in forms more compatible with twenty-first-century technologies and ideologies."[48] Inflected differently, James demonstrates that sonically oriented theoretical approaches too often prescribe under the guise of description, and in so doing naturalize the ontological foundations of contemporary power relations. If sound, resonance, and even listening are to be productive models for theorizing, then they must model "intellectual and social practices that are designed to avoid and/or oppose the systemic relations of domination that classical liberalism and neoliberalism create."[49]

There is a pragmatic dimension to this insight, in that it weds the meanings of propositions to what they actually do. In that spirit (and in light of James's argument), this book adopts a double stance toward listening: it asks what we might learn from listening to data incommunicatively, but also how might we go about doing so in ways that listen to listening differently in order to tune into the strange aesthetic affordances that come with transducing the unvisualizably immense scales of contemporary data practices (which are themselves transductive abstractions, like real estate is). Since, in the following pages, I often approach these questions according to specifically pragmatic protocols, a brief gloss of that thinking may be warranted (even if an extended scholarly engagement with pragmatism proper is beyond both the scope and commitments of this book). In short, pragmatism is an experimental theory of knowledge that dissolves the opposition between theory and practice that appears in other approaches, as well as that between appearance and reality. Likewise, metaphysical paradoxes tend to be cast aside, as there is a general rejection—through what is called the pragmatic maxim—of the notion that there are facts that are unknowable in principle. As discussed in chapter 1, the perceived opposition between ontology and epistemology is also immaterial. In this sense, pragmatism is akin to religious agnosticism: just as for the agnostic the very question of the existence of divinity isn't sensible in its own right, so for the pragmatist such questions are not properly askable.

If the conditions for being able to ask such questions are not available, we can nonetheless interrogate the stakes of answering them: we can ask what is really being claimed when an untenable claim is made. The stakes of pragmatism are thus themselves pragmatic in that it is an approach that stays close to the question of who/what a given utterance is in service, as well as the correlative questions of exclusion. Glosses of pragmatism often

14   Introduction

state that there must be a practical difference tied to the truth or falsehood of a proposition in order for it to be part of a genuine (i.e., rather than simply semantic) disagreement or problem; while this is true as far as it goes, I prefer to emphasize the ways that a pragmatic approach palpates the work of a proposition—what it does. In this, a pragmatic attentiveness bends our ears toward the ongoing production of differences as they act in the world, including the weights, forces, speeds, and redirections that they add to actual situations.

Many of the ideas in this book were born in the midst of precisely such specificities, developed as they were from pragmatic methods: readers will no doubt note that many of the argumentative strains in this book are carried by artistic and technical engagements that I myself undertook. Such practices are, for me, integral to staying with the trouble of signals' morethans: this is the case because it helps me focus not only on the technical affordances and constraints of a given situation but also on the ways that these technicalities are actually and constitutively caught up in social, semiotic, and historical realities that both exceed and condition them. The situatedness of artistic and technical practices is real. Hence, I share elements of my own creative practice in this book not because I think the resulting artworks are important in an art historical sense (I resolutely don't think this), but rather because these practices are lived in tandem—literally coproductively—with the ideas about which I'm writing.

There are evident parallels between pragmatic philosophy and contemporary, nonessentialist understandings of sound (and, relatedly, listening). The first chapter of this book—"Networking Sound and Medium Specificity"—prepares the ground for the pragmatically conceptual understandings of listening that feature throughout the monograph by working through questions and stakes of medium specificity as they relate to sound. In service of this argument, the chapter extensively discusses a custom software tool and internet-based artwork—*Exurbia* (2011–14), created by myself and William Brent—that leverages a strange pragmatics of sound against existing understandings of specific forms of network communication. *Exurbia* is characterized by four distinct features:

- the interface is time intensive, being predominantly aural and executed in real time;

- editing is destructive (i.e., there is no "undo" feature);

- all source materials (i.e., sound samples) are shared among all users, but are used to produce discrete pieces; and

- each edit on a single user's computer impacts every instance of a single file throughout the *Exurbia* community (i.e., the materials are dislocated).

As I argue, the particular way in which these features are brought together in *Exurbia* results in a work that undermines the equation of networks with exchange and the prioritization of data over relations, while affording a strange, aurally modulated individual compositional experience that is in important senses secondary to the experience of an online community: experience itself is felt in its relational dimension, untethered from the presumptions of individuality.

Chapter 2—"Listening and Technicity"—extends this engagement with sound to the disposition of listening, specifically in a way that acknowledges the technicity that obtains in listening (whether a computer is involved or not). Focusing this engagement is a discussion of the wearable technology Fathead, a device that variously simulates how it might sound to have a one-thousand-foot-wide head. Crucially, the chapter not only attends to Fathead as a prosthetic technology but also details the work's development in order to tease out its more obscure potentials as a device for palpating the role of experiential (in)variance in knowledge sharing. In this way, the chapter attunes less to what listening is and more to the ways that elaborations of listening's technical assemblages can disclose and even be productive of different incommunicative registers.

In some respects the heart of the book, chapter 3—"Incomputable and Integral Incommunications"—further interrogates the collective experiential knots that are textured by the specific technical relations of listening by asking how the machinations of computers specifically impact their processing of sound, and what can we learn from this. To answer these questions, I closely consider the recent work of M. Beatrice Fazi on incomputability (and, to a lesser extent, Wolfgang Ernst's concept of time criticality), which parses a constitutive contingency that is internal to computation. From this reading, I proceed to consider the Fourier integral—the function from which sound (re)synthesis derives—in its contingent potentials in order to map a terrain of processual computational excesses that operate incommunicatively even as they cannot be accounted for in the logic of computation proper.

The excesses that chapter 3 explains are pressured for their aesthetic affordances in the art practices discussed in chapter 4—"Algorithms, Art, and Sonicity"—especially in their production of strange temporalities that emerge alongside the interscalar relations that digital technologies privilege. Moreover, in this chapter I demonstrate how listening affords a specific position in these encounters. With its characteristic coupling of human activity with unthinkable machinic speeds and scales, contemporary technoculture intensifies the basic but essential incommunicative problem of how to act responsibly when one's actions are implicated in nonlinear networks that exceed the purview of consciousness. In this chapter, I listen alongside the ways that art has textured this bind by bringing aesthetic practices to bear on digital technologies (and to the algorithms through which they operate), specifically attending to works by Colin Clark, Kelly Egan, Shilpa Gupta, Ryoji Ikeda, Renee Lear, Evan Merz, and Juliana Pivato. Importantly, this situates listening as a not-necessarily-sonic experience, working from the position that it is not only possible to listen to visual processes, but it is arguably necessary to develop nonvisual techniques for steering human-technology coupling—of becoming agential through distributed attunement—in order to address the unvisualizably immense and minute scales that subtend so many contemporary experiences. The aesthetic component of this address is a crucial technique for denaturalizing the logics at work in these experiences that come to fruition in the sonic episteme, and provides the ground for a critique of creative capitalism by insisting on something that remains inexchangeable.

The final chapter of the book—"Listening and Technicity (Once and for All, Again and Again)"—is perhaps the book's strangest and most adventurous, unfolding the relational, mediatic, and multicausal logics of incommunication in settings ranging from basketball and squash courts to video games to dreams and intuitions. I begin this chapter by working again through the technics of listening, but this time with a rigorous ear for the experiential (in the full, distributed sense of the term) that would not have been coherent without the earlier chapters. From this grounding, I work through several examples of the (a)systematic, extra-auditory operations of (incommunicational) listening, and especially those that leverage the productive powers of adjacency that come with collectivities. Through these examples, the incommunication thesis that both motivates and captures so much of this book becomes—if still not quite graspable—as legible as it can ever be, charting a multiverse of never-quite-possible actualities that may nonetheless (in a different sense) be fated. If, as I argue above, the impossibility of communication abounds both once and for all and also again and again, this closing chapter demonstrates how that paradox forms a resonant frequency through which relations attune. (Though pitched in a different register altogether, this is also the aim of the postscript.)

To summarize, *Listening in the Afterlife of Data* begins by accepting that communication isn't actually possible, which is an observation that every communicative discipline has at least partially acknowledged. By accepting this at the outset, I am able to more clearly think through the ways that communication, as a metaphor, seduces us into certain assumptions, affording certain sorts of activities while constraining others. Even knowing that *communication* is a radically fictitious term, it circulates apparitionally in and as the afterlife of data: that is, it remains remarkably difficult to avoid falling into the habits of thinking-acting that imagine information to be something that is passed, unchanged, between senders and receivers. The ubiquity of computation marks the ascendance of this metaphor of communication to a hegemonic position. The effective equation today is simple: for the most part, communication = computation = data = exchangeability. That this equation evinces a thoroughly impoverished understanding of relations as they actually exist has had little bearing on its usability. Of course it matters that the word *communication* doesn't just mean consumer computing technologies, but it also matters that for many people, much of the time, it does (even as computation remains metaphorical).

Incommunication, then, is about hijacking the communicative metaphor, wrestling its undeniable powers of (cultural) production from the iconography of computation. Data is never really a representational mediation of experience, but rather is an incommunicative thing that finds itself in a complex relation between the possibility of universalizing (computational) abstraction and the necessity of living and perceiving upon singular (or particular) experiential grounds. By shifting the metaphor to incommunication—by working from and through the incoherence of universals and particulars—we can pervert the established orthodoxy of interpreting rela-

18   Introduction

tions in the digital age through the tired metaphor of the network, opening up new investigative avenues in media studies.[50]

Listening—understood beyond its mere sensory implications—is the mode in which this book undertakes such investigations, not because listening has somehow been culturally suppressed (it hasn't been) but because it is a metaphor that is particularly suited to engaging these notions of exchange. As discussed above, this suitability is itself Janus-faced insofar as sonic metaphors align with those of the market, so that to critique listening is, in part, to pull apart the founding assumptions of the particular form of neoliberalism that computation naturalizes and intensifies—especially as computation migrates to artificial intelligence, moving toward a moment when computation will have fully hegemonized our cultural understanding of knowledge even as it has entirely shed its skin of recognizable, hardware computers.

To listen in the afterlife of data is thus a pragmatic undertaking, approaching communication, listening, and data by asking what practical and material differences their figurations make, to whom, and most importantly how. I am not advocating a redefinition of these concepts, but instead describing the ways that they are—like all concepts—lived, and thus open to nudges that would have us live them otherwise. That is, *Listening in the Afterlife of Data* joins a growing body of literature that suspends the question of definition in favor of asking what experience can do: "whats" have always also been "hows," and I'm curious if the psychedelic incoherence of this claim can be taken a little more seriously with respect to communication. Certainly, the artworks, experiments, scenes, and stories that I take up all open onto such definitional excesses; can thought, in its theoretical profile, also do so?

Introduction   19

1

Networking Sound and Medium Specificity

In order to approach the question of how we might listen to computers in their incommunicative profiles, we will need to understand what is entailed in listening—and before moving to listening, it behooves us to consider something of the medium specificity of sound. Since medium specificity has been a central and thorny concern in aesthetic discourse's contact with artistic practice, we might learn something from engaging the topic specifically in the context of music and sound art. In order to do so, over the course of this chapter I engage Seth Kim-Cohen's call for a noncochlear sound art based on the notion of "expansion" that has been decisive in visual arts discourses. I argue that Kim-Cohen's noncochlear intervention in *In the Blink of an Ear* (2009) might be productively pressured toward an understanding of the material-discursive particularity of sound that doesn't make recourse to the phenomenological claims of authenticity that Kim-Cohen (correctly) abhors. In service of this argument, the chapter extensively discusses a sound and media artwork—*Exurbia* (2011–14), created by myself and William Brent—that leverages the metaphorics of sound against conventional understandings of network communication. I argue that the conceptual and material dimensions of the project stridulate in a hum of recursive vectors for reconfiguring the constitution and consequences of networked aural interaction. *Exurbia* can thus be parsed in terms of medium specificity precisely because its digital aural materials are themselves also something else. That is, *Exurbia* demonstrates how the medium incommunicates, where its conceptual and material aspects (in)cohere in practice. From this, I argue more generally that to listen to music as music is to hear it as a form of incommunication.

$$\frac{x}{2} = \frac{x}{200}$$

At first glance, this equation may seem incorrect.[1] After all, how can a number divided by 2 be equivalent to the same number divided by 200? Of course, not only is the statement not impossible, it is actually possible to solve for x almost instantaneously, without the machinations of calculation or any contextual information: the only possible solution is $x = 0$.

Notably, zero is an utterly abstract number in the sense that it does not make even secondary reference to a concrete material base. Thus, while the number two (for example) also doesn't refer to anything we can apprehend with our senses, it is at least apparent how the number's abstraction is theoretically tied to the empirical world; we can't imagine "the two itself," but we can imagine two apples, two cars, two options, and so on, such that we can functionally connect the items in the list through their "twoness." This is not the case for zero, which is utterly foreign to physical, positivist reality.

The point is, if the variable x doesn't indicate anything that at least subtends a concrete system of thinking (wherein x may be abstract, but it is an abstraction of some physical thing that we can at least feign grasping), the details of the surrounding material are precluded from any impact: 2 might as well be equivalent to 200. In order to maintain their specificity, the details depend on the status of the variable because it is the variable x that is invariant in the equation. If x is not understood as being, a priori, a positive substantial element, then we are unable to logically deduce a difference between 2 and 200.

If, on the other hand, we reach beyond the equation itself to limit x to being a nonzero number, then we have the inverse problem, namely that

$\frac{x}{y} = \frac{x}{z}$ only if $y = z$.[2] The problem here is that if y and z are the same, then the equation is really just the tautology $\frac{x}{y} = \frac{x}{y}$. Taken together, then, these equations suggest that without the possibility of unlimited abstraction, the limited abstraction—the ability to reach beyond its grasp—that any logical, denotative relation depends on becomes tied to its own particular circumstance and thereby loses its prescriptive power. A tautology by definition tells us nothing about the system or circumstances that exceed it, so while we can take note of tautologies, we cannot reason from them.

Taken together, we can generalize the problem that this equation points to as a problem of medium specificity in the arts. That is, attempting to make a claim about a medium x requires one to either abstract that medium from direct experience (as in the first reading of our exemplary equation) or impose an otherwise arbitrary constraint on what counts as the medium, which can only lead to confirmation of the constraint's applicability in a given instance rather than to a statement about the medium itself (i.e., if it is true, it will be tautological). Simply put, an aesthetic medium such as sound, paint, stone, and so on must always point beyond itself in order to articulate itself as an integral system, as something about which one can make a substantial claim. It is both necessary and impossible to insist on medium specificity.

This problem is familiar to visual arts scholars, particularly through the notion of "expansion" elaborated by Rosalind Krauss in the context of sculpture and Gene Youngblood with respect to cinema.[3] Related to différance as it is outlined in Derridean grammatology, expansion is a means of recognizing the porousness of an artwork's boundaries; the implicit verb in any frame (that is, a frame is a framing, as Mieke Bal would have it);[4] and the entanglement of artworks, culture, and discourse.[5] As Clement Greenberg puts it, the work of a work is not wholly reducible to the boundaries of the work itself, and neither are those boundaries themselves uncontested or fixed.

While this line of thinking is old hat in the various discourses that make up the visual arts, it remains only peripheral to the dominant discourses of music and sound art. With respect to the institutionalized form of music that is problematically captured by the term "concert music," this is perhaps not surprising. There is, first of all, a foundational social conservatism in such music drawn from its colonial and sacred histories. More relevant to this conversation, though, is the medial purity that music is endowed with through its constitution as music: Walter Pater's (in)famous and oft-repeated claim that "all art constantly aspires to the condition of music" perfectly encapsulates the fiction of music as an abstraction in the first sense of our equation, relating to nothing but itself.[6] That is, Pater's claim posits music as the purest of the arts precisely because its "artness" makes reference only to itself, functioning acontextually and asemiotically. Seth Kim-Cohen points out that this perception is discursively reinforced by the fact that "only music includes, as part of its discursive vocabulary, a term for the foreign matter threatening always to infect it: 'the extramusical.'"[7]

Of course, not even a musician (especially not a musician!) would claim that concert music is entirely cut off from the world, and indeed even according to the most idealistic understanding the musical project would necessarily include some means for music to affect beyond itself. The point, though, is that this affecting is not always considered part of music "proper" or "the music itself," but rather what music "does."[8] What is indicated, then, is an insulation that is constructed via the rhetoric of music.[9] Thus, it isn't the case that concert music—to the extent that it results from this genealogy—misapprehends itself as a kind of fixed, extradiscursive object, lacking a sense of its own contingency (as such a reading would miss the crucial aspiration of Pater's claim), but rather that concert music aligns with the way that the modernist (visual) art project is often characterized, which is to say as evading "'objecthood' . . . by being the active (or enacted) site of internal relations" instead of including the external world within its purview.[10]

What makes this a problem for concert music—and indeed, for concert music in general rather than just for specific musical works—is that the transubstantiation of sound into music takes place precisely via the activation or summoning of this rhetoric. The problem thus takes the tautological form of our opening equation: the rhetoric of music—which consists in the fiction that time is shaped into a succession of sounds that can be situated on a continuum of musical meaning—is not conceived as supplementing a material base that is already musical, but instead is the very music that it promotes. Put differently, something is musical to the extent that it participates in a rhetoric of music—that is, in the form of meaning making that is particular to music—but this rhetoric, precisely because it is particular to music, only comes to be from something being musical. In this view, music comes about only when sounds are made musically meaningful. In this sense music is simulational, making reference only to itself.

The point I am working toward is that one cannot address problems of music and discourse by simply expanding music's semantic field. In the language of second-order systems theory, music can catalyze and be catalyzed by extramusical factors, but it cannot cause them; that is, music can activate (and be activated by) social, cultural, and political valences, but to the extent that these factors operate via logics that exceed those of music—and vice versa—a systematic distinction remains operative.[11] To characterize the rhetorical (e.g., notated) details of a piece of music (as opposed to the practices and institutions that collect around it) as meaningful is a project that is both necessary (to sustain the implicit value that it is necessary to invest in music) and doomed to fail in advance (because musical details are constituted tautologically, in and through their disconnection from the extramusical world). As I will return to shortly, music's medium specificity will always risk confirming (without necessarily confirming) its apolitical valence, which is as sure a sign as any of a subsumption of agencies into a preexistent politics that is indifferent to local details.[12] That is, like any rhetoric that appears to possess closed borders of signification (i.e., to be constitutively insulated), the genealogy of music that flows through Pater has in fact simply naturalized the porousness of its boundaries. To the extent that (as Kim-Cohen writes, paraphrasing Derrida) "there is no extra-music,"[13] it necessarily follows that there is also no music proper. Put bluntly, it is not just that only music musicks, but also that not even music musicks—this incommunicative paradox is how music (in)coheres.

The decisive—and most frequently referenced—example here is the work of John Cage, which would seem to deploy the very expanded field that, I am arguing, music cannot avow. That is, Cage's extensive use of aleatoricism and his positivistic technologization of silence are each in service of an understanding that would move music off the page and beyond the purview of an intentional composerly rhetoric. Quite simply, Cage's intervention expands the musical palette to include sounds that are "physically uniquely themselves" independent of their notation, completely liberated from "abstract ideas about them."[14]

However, while such gestures broaden the rhetorical palette available to musicians and constitute an important musical politics in themselves, they do not impact its purview. That is, the expansive inclusivity of such practice is accomplished via a colonizing process that in no way addresses the discursive insularity that prevents music from avowing its contingency.

This is the case because an enormously problematic assumption lies at the heart of Cage's project, namely, that sound signifies itself. Thus, as Eldritch Priest argues,

> Cage's effort to open musical experience to a wider materiality . . . could only be made effective through a rhetorical manoeuvre that ciphered the semiotic remainders of sound first through the measure of duration and then through the supposed paradoxical intentionality of silence. . . . Any sound was musical so long as it was intentionally heard as music and *un-heard* in its worldliness. That is, sounds are musical to the extent that their being-heard articulates the intentions that constitute the traditional horizon of listening musically while at the same time seeming to disarticulate those intentions that tradition places on the composer.[15]

Douglas Kahn famously made a similar point in the late 1990s, influentially noting that "under the guise of a new aurality, an opening up to the sounds of the world, Cage built a musical bulwark against auditive culture, one founded on a musical identification with nature itself."[16] Kahn demonstrates convincingly that this was accomplished precisely through the techniques that Cage shared with visual arts discourses of expansion: Cage extended the process of musical incorporation to include all audible, potentially audible, and mythically audible sounds, until "there existed no more sounds to incorporate into music, and [he had] formalized the performance of music to where it could be dependent on listening alone."[17]

In short, the medium specificity of sound mobilized in and as the rhetoric of music acts as our variable x, so that additional elements (y and z) that are brought into relation with its redoubled abstraction do so only to the extent that they give up what is elemental to them. In practice, then, music can never be medium specific, since its specificity exists only prior to any particular instantiation of it. Or, by the same logic, music can only be medium specific, which amounts to the same thing: if music is only music in the sense (pace Cage) that music is only what we hear when we decide that what we're listening to is music, then it's not only the case that particular instances of music can't be medium specific (since even Cagean music would have to be defined according and in relation to something that is not music, i.e., a listener), but also that music must be medium specific if it

26   Chapter One

is to be conceptualized and conceptually expanded (i.e., if even Cage is to speak of it as a limited concept that requires expansion).

In sum, to consider the medium specificity of music is to engage it as incommunication. As with our opening equation, the problem that music poses requires either an arbitrarily prescribed limit to the problem or an acceptance of a certain tautology. As may be seen in the broadening of subject matter that has obtained in musicology since at least the 1980s, sustaining this problem as a problem requires at once a means of registering that of a given musical practice which simultaneously must and cannot be particular, as well as the excesses—performative and incommunicative—of which this conundrum is productive. Put differently, one must approach the problem of music pragmatically.

To speak of the medium specificity of music is as fraught as speaking of the truth of painting, sculpture, photography, and so on. A fascinating distinction —or perhaps difference of emphasis—develops in the case of music, though. In the visual arts, the constitutive entanglement of works with that which exceeds them has been largely addressed through a turn toward conceptualism (in the broad sense) that explicitly and practically engages the paradoxical ways in which the discursive valences that subtend works also constitute them.[18] Concert music, on the other hand, has dealt with its excesses through sound art, which "as a discrete practice, is . . . the remainder created by music closing off its borders to the extramusical," the parole that cannot be "comfortably expressed in the *langue* of the Western notational system."[19] Again, though, this is not the result of different decisions by different actors within the respective discourses: because a certain approach to music defines it exclusively through its internal workings—because concert music is always in an important sense "pure music," even though it never is—there is no other option available.[20]

The problem is not so easily solved, though, even from the perspective of sound art. Returning to Cage, Kahn notes the bracketing out of discourse in the apocryphal myth of the anechoic chamber that animates so much of his reception: in addition to the two sounds Cage hears—allegedly that of his nervous system and of his blood circulating, though this has been contested—Kahn notes a third, namely, Cage's internal voice asking what the two sounds he is hearing are. This is a crucial insight because "such quasi-sounds were, of course, antithetical to Cagean listening by being in competition with *sounds in themselves,* yet here he was able to listen and at the same time allow discursiveness to intrude in the experience."[21] Indeed, one could go a step further to insist that insofar as hearing and listening can be distinguished along the lines of concentration, to listen is to listen discursively.[22] Moreover—and in order to preclude counterarguments constructed around notions like meditative or deep listening—we should note that this also means that to have listened is to listen discursively.

One needn't plant a flag in the (often vitriolic) ontology/epistemology debate in order to recognize that language is a central technology through which experience is registered as such, and indeed one shouldn't: it is true in a sense that we know things only through language, but the term *language* in this statement greatly exceeds mere text. Deconstruction is not a theory of textuality, but rather a theory of media and meaning, of which literal textuality is but a subvariety.[23] As such, language and experience are always already materially enmeshed with one another (whatever else they might be). Such is a pragmatic position, forwarding an antirealist materialism: since "materialism is an ontological thesis that posits that being can be independent of thinking . . . and realism posits the thinkability of this being independent of thinking," one can "maintain a materialist standpoint . . . that the entity and the real are ontologically prior to thought, while denying the direct and immediate access of thought to such an entity."[24] When Derrida says "there is no world," then, he doesn't mean it in the sense of the world not being real but in the sense of a philosophically realist account of the world not being real.[25] Likewise, recognizing that there is "no music proper" denies music per se (literally, "in itself"), but advances a musical pragmatics.

Emphatically, then, the soft claim that listening and discourse are always already interwoven yields the hard (Derridean) pragmatic claim against what Kim-Cohen calls the "essentialist reading of the two great bestowals of Cage and [Pierre] Schaeffer—silence-as-sound and sound-in-itself."[26] That is, Kim-Cohen criticizes a number of sound art practices that leverage transduction into and out of the medium of sound for being "based on faith in a fundamental stratum of experience, on some essential ontological state, a metaphysics."[27] Thus, for example, he criticizes Rainer Maria Rilke's fantasy of playing the groove of a coronal suture with a phonographic stylus in order to articulate its "primal sound" for its implication that "there is a completeness in nature and that our sense of incomplete experience . . . is a product of our inadequate perceptual faculties."[28] As Kim-Cohen notes, this perspective—which aligns with the broader neo-Romantic sensibility that is made explicit in Rilke's poetry, but remains implicit in numerous sound art practices that feature similar transductions—is predicated on a belief in the type of foundational metaphysics that Derridean grammatology so thoroughly deconstructs.

Notably, Kim-Cohen's reading of Rilke is motivated directly against that of Friedrich Kittler, from whom the example is drawn in service of an argument that "sense perceptions are revealed as nothing more than neutral data flows."[29] While an extensive engagement with Kittler is beyond the scope of my argument, I will note that the connection that Kim-Cohen draws between sound art and Kittler's "interest in authorless media streams" anticipates the way I discuss *Exurbia* in the final section of this chapter.[30] Kim-Cohen's assertion that "contextless data is gobbledygook" aligns with *Exurbia*'s investigation of sound and networks, which pragmatically poses the question of how the relation of the two informs both and helps us resist totalizing them under the respective signs of their nomination (i.e., the network and the sound itself).[31]

An implicit question is posed by Kim-Cohen's call for greater acknowledgment of the discursive vectors that are active in sound art practices and that make authentic self-presence impossible. Simply put: if sound art loses recourse to any kind of sonic authenticity—that is, to an extradiscursive, categorical, a priori difference between sound and other sensorial experiences such as vision—and is entirely captured in discourse in the same way that the gallery arts are, what distinctions remain? Can sonic practices be distinguished from visual ones? Should they be? And to what would such a distinction be in service?

While *In the Blink of an Ear* offers an important intervention into the rapidly proliferating discussions of sound art, it is perhaps a shortcoming of the book that few examples are given that might address these questions. One example that is given, however, is compelling: consider the insightful reading that Kim-Cohen offers of Jarrod Fowler's *Kosuth to Fowler* (2006), a piece that works with Joseph Kosuth's *Text/Context* (1979) as its source material. As Kim-Cohen recounts, the original (Kosuth) work consists of "two adjacent outdoor public billboards [that] display related texts referring to each other and to their respective methods of linguistic and visual communication."[32] In Fowler's treatment, the text's visual indicators (such as "see" and "text/sign") are changed to corresponding acoustic ones (such as "hear" and "speech/recording") and are "then read by a speech synthesizer, with the left text on the left side of the stereo field, the right text on the right."[33] Kim-Cohen notes that "the simultaneous transmission of the two texts accomplishes something that would be impossible with Kosuth's original," namely, the erasure of the "literal and essential" space between the two texts.[34]

The provenance of this productive difference is underemphasized by Kim-Cohen, though, which is perhaps a symptom of the book's avowed movement toward a noncochlear sound art and presumably away from the pragmatic medium specificities of sound. That is, while it is impossible to insist on something like "the sound itself," it nonetheless remains the case that certain characteristics flow more readily from certain materials; there are material-semiotic differences, after all, between sound and vision, and it behooves us to be careful not to collapse these distinctions under the sign of discourse as though the latter meant something fixed and concrete. We can note, then, that there is a danger in Kim-Cohen's reading of *Kosuth to Fowler* of implicitly prioritizing the similarity of the text that the piece shares with its source material over the different media that distribute it.[35] This raises the question: how would one work through an analogous reading without invoking the alibi of shared material created by the amedial legibility of text, an alibi that is dangerously proximate to the notion that material can be passed between media without being changed? Simply put, if we treated the text exclusively as information (which it undoubtedly is, though not entirely), one could (mis)construct Kim-Cohen's reading of this piece as assuming precisely the type of metaphysical underpinning that he criticizes in Rilke and Kittler. How, then, can the work be read incommunicatively?

This is a subtle point, and doesn't entirely oppose Kim-Cohen's reading. In fact, he points in this direction by highlighting the fact that Fowler engages the Kosuth piece not only by appropriating its literal content—which would be the informational quality of the text, as opposed to what we might call its signifying capacity—but also by intervening in the conceptual field that the work constructs. He argues, for example, that the simultaneity of the Fowler "problematizes the cross-referentiality of the two texts" in the Kosuth.[36] What I am pointing to, though, is a pragmatic insistence that is

30   Chapter One

often stressed by systems theorists such as Niklas Luhmann: whereas deconstruction emphasizes the final undecidability of any signifying instance, systems nonetheless decide.[37]

What this points to, then, is the incommunicative dimension of deconstruction, which is an integral dimension that is regularly neglected. Put differently, deconstruction is pragmatically performative; that is, the Derridean claim is not so much that all experiences partake of language's instability and ambiguity, but more that our knowledge of them does (and that they come to be for us only through becoming objects of knowledge). As a result, the inverse is also true: Derridean claims about language are predicated precisely on language's being understood not as a system that is closed off from the world but rather as a contingent systemizing that constructs a border that is always already seeping through with that which it excludes. That is, extrapolating a process into an observational register (or a predictive or categorical one, for that matter) in order to delve into its meaning is not a neutral endeavor: understanding a process as a process, rather than as a random or even stochastic set of events, necessarily presumes a frame of reference. The paradoxical logic of grammatology is performative in the precise sense that every constative claim enacts something supplementary to itself. Moreover, this supplement is qualitatively different from that which it claims, and is thus enacted precisely insofar as it fails to be.

This performative dimension of incommunication that deconstruction has so scrupulously (if often obscurely) limned is crucial because it marks a vector of material specificity—even as that specificity remains under erasure—through which we can insist on the particular implications of aural experience without validating the authenticity of that experience, provided we keep in mind that the economy of such experiences is incommunicative. As Jonathan Sterne argues, understanding the faculty of audition requires understanding not only its "status as embedded in real social relations [but also] its power as a figurative and imaginative metaphor."[38] In this light, claiming that sound's "phenomenal characteristics—the fact that it is invisible, intangible, ephemeral, and vibrational—coordinate with the physiology of the ears to create a perceptual experience profoundly different from the dominant sense of sight" does not undermine Kim-Cohen's noncochlear orientation, but rather redoubles it: it takes the materiality of discourse seriously enough to insist not only that all experience is discursive, but also that the paradoxical quality of this discursiveness necessarily produces "extradiscursive" experiences as part and parcel of its movements.[39] That is, experience is neither reduced nor constructed by language, but intensified as experience even and especially as such experience is under erasure.

Returning to the question of the material specificity of sound, we might speak instead of a "sonic pragmatism" in order to emphasize a contingent operational frame. In this understanding, "sonic materiality operates as 'micro-epistemologies,' with the echo, the vibration, the rhythmic, for instance, opening up specific ways of knowing the world," so that we might provisionally sidestep ontological questions about sound without sacrificing our engagement with its unique material capacities.[40] That is, a pragmatic emphasis invokes an incommunicative perspective that articulates the double bind of the opening equation of this chapter as a necessary element—a necessary impossibility, if you will—of the ongoing and ever-changing articulation of a sound/nonsound difference. By framing the problem in this manner, we can eschew any definition of sound but nonetheless maintain the validity of questions pertaining to the unique intensities that instances of aurality—like all instances—caress. In this way, we can at least postpone directly equating sound art with the other gallery arts, which would be to throw the baby out with the bathwater: even if language equally conditions what is thinkable across media, the effect of a perceived heightened abstraction in sound is no less real. Appearances matter, as do their seductions. The task becomes one of describing these "extradiscursive" effects in their discursivity, which is to say in such a way that they incommunicatively couple with other metaphors. Such a task is not undertaken in the interest of reducing them to conceptual practices that are already familiar to us, but rather in the interest of catalyzing new forms of nonsense, new vectors of incommunicative recursion. In short, thinking through sonic pragmatism is an attempt to avow the incommunicative dimensions of sound in their absolute nonuniversality.

This is the context in which I'd like to discuss *Exurbia*, which explicitly pressures a pragmatic understanding of sound as it obtains in the context of contemporary digital networked communities. What I hope to show is a way of activating sound's (contingent) medium specificity, of putting it into play in order to learn something about both digital networks and aurality that we might not have known without their coupling. If these lessons remain contingent on the local instances of the metaphors that they mobilize (i.e., sound and digital networks), they will be all the more potent for it. In *Exurbia*, then, the incommunicative bind of $\frac{x}{y} = \frac{x}{z}$ is explicitly sustained precisely as such: in line with the mathematical investments integral to the historical development of computation, the question of equivalence—catalyzed but not captured by the = symbol—is taken to indicate a "finite, dynamic *sense*" rather than an "infinite, static denotation."[41]

Put simply, *Exurbia* is a digital sound-editing program that has four distinct features:

- the interface is time intensive, being predominantly aural and executed in real time (as opposed to a static, visual-spatial interface);

- editing is destructive (i.e., there is no undo feature);

- all of the source materials (i.e., the sound samples) are shared among all users, but are used to produce discrete pieces; and

- each edit on a single user's computer impacts every instance of a single file throughout the *Exurbia* community (i.e., the materials are dislocated).

Taken together, these features introduce a reflexive component to the otherwise practically oriented environment that to my mind situates it as a creative work in its own right, rather than as a software tool. That is, *Exurbia* is an environment that is oriented toward composing musical works, but it is equally directed toward an engagement with the process of musical composition itself as it obtains in an aurally intensive networked digital environment.

In essence, the piece works as follows: participants navigate to a website where they can download the program, upload short sound samples to a communal pool, and/or listen to other users' contributions (both samples and pieces that have been composed using the program). After downloading, users open the program and authorize it to synchronize with the current batch of sound samples that are on the server, a process that can take up to five minutes and is necessary each time the program is opened.

Once the files are synchronized, participants can then begin using the program, which is done by loading any individual sample file and applying any combination of twelve different parametric modifications to it (including multiple iterations of a single modification).[42] Unlike in conventional editing programs, each time that a modification is applied the entire sample is played, and the majority of the modifiers feature parameters that are controlled in real time using a mouse. Thus, for example, if a user wishes to increase the volume of a sample midway through it, they must select the appropriate modifier and sample, play the sample, and ramp up the volume slider with the mouse at the appropriate time. Since there is no undo feature, if participants are not happy with the outcome they can only reverse the effects of the modification by attempting the same process, but attenuating the volume rather than increasing it.[43]

When a user has finished editing a given sample, they insert it into a master track (which is completely unique to each user) by entering a start time in seconds into a number box; each time a sample is inserted, the entire master track is played. Notably—and, again, unlike in most digital editing programs—there are no editing options beyond these insertions: samples cannot be removed or reedited after insertion, and no global adjustments such as master volume boosts or attenuations are possible.

Crucially, inserting an edited sample replaces all instances of a sample in the collective source material with the one that has just been edited. This means that the changes apply equally to the piece that the local composer is working on and to the compositions of other users. This substitution, however, does not take place until the participant finishes their editing session and shuts down the program, so that it is entirely possible that a user might overwrite material in their own composition without realizing it until the next time they open the program.

The sample that is to be replaced is determined by the program in a predictable series, and is indicated by the time in which the sample to be edited was selected. As such, participants who do not want to alter every instance of a given sample have the option of gaming the system by substituting an inaudibly edited version of the same sample as that which is to be replaced.[44] This is a cumbersome process, but one that allows a degree of preservation from the consequences of one's compositional actions in the environment.

Indeed, while it is not possible to insulate one's composition from the activities of others, it is possible to (imperfectly) predict how editing activities will affect others' compositions and act accordingly. This requires a certain kind of listening. That is, participants always have the option of listening to the most recently saved version of others' pieces (finished or in progress) from within the program environment, so that one can get a sense of how substantially one's edits will affect other works. This is, again, cumbersome, as it can only be accomplished by listening to the works (i.e., there is no textual component that would tell a person what files are being used), which can only take place in real time. Compositions created in *Exurbia* are also audible online for nonusers.

It is precisely these technical machinations that constitute *Exurbia*'s intervention into the alibi of the sound itself that is naturalized in digital technologies. As I discuss throughout this book, a central conceptual gambit of the computer is to persuade us to think of everything as communicable data, which is to say as extradiscursive content composed of discrete, manipulable, exchangeable units. This very much extends to sound, which is conceptualized in precisely these terms as it is typically presented on computational devices. By working in real time, *Exurbia* undermines the implicit fixity of this materiality, an undermining that is further emphasized through the program's collective siting of its materials, as well as by the way that it conflates the process of creating with the creative outcomes. Consider again: any alteration of a sample requires a complete, real-time reiteration of the sample, and this reiteration by definition alters the broader context of the sample's articulation (by overwriting another sample that exists elsewhere) such that the outcome of the edit exceeds the desired change that precedes it within both the individual composition and the broader community. In short, *Exurbia* disrupts the injunction to categorize that is implicit in the quotidian notion of data by emphasizing the excesses and slippages that are constitutive of categories insofar as the latter are always reiterative. It also palpates an incommunicative vector of data sharing by constituting the data relationally rather than discretely, raising the question of how the notion of data sharing would need to change if data were taken to be first and constitutively a relational phenomenon.

Exurbia's mobilization of sonic pragmatism is in this sense an incommunicative intervention, one that amounts to a participatory quasi-experience of digital musical (non)composition that is fundamentally different from the way that sound is typically treated in digital settings. If the interface is cumbersome, then—and even if, in some senses, *Exurbia* is a failed work as a result—these impediments to smooth usage are as much positive markers of the work's difference as they are indications of its failure to actualize.[45]

At the center of *Exurbia*'s conceptual gambit is an obvious downplaying of visual graphics and other forms of data visualization, most notably manifested through the absence of visible sound waves. In this, the work explicitly contrasts related editing programs (Pro Tools, GarageBand, Audacity, Logic, etc.) that are built around visualized waveforms as their basic interface for manipulating sounds. In constructing objects that can be manipulated according to their own instantaneous logics of manipulation, such programs spatialize the temporal element of sound. Thus, for example, a waveform editor treats a stereo output in ways that are inconceivable in real-time acoustic settings; that is, as a composition of independent sound files that can easily and almost instantaneously be recombined, disarticulated, stretched, reversed, compressed, moved, muted, paused, and so on, as though the piece is an object or an image on the screen.

To be clear, this is not to say that waveform editing somehow robs sound of an essential quality, but rather points to the way that sound—which, again, is always already so constitutively entangled that it can only be invoked as a shorthand—is constructed in the context of the computer's metamedial metaphorics, which is to say by the computer's invitation to think of media as interchangeable through the language of ones and zeros. In this way, waveform editors invite a conception of sound that aligns with the dominant (visual) paradigm of the computer wherein the informational content of a message—in a definition of information famously inherited from Claude Shannon—is literally divorced from its content. Data—the lingua franca of the computer, and a synonym for information on the computer—is atemporal in the precise sense that it is constitutively contextless: data is that which can be moved from one setting to the next, seemingly without being changed.

This atemporality of data is of course not an extradiscursive fact, but rather constitutes the fiction through which human-computer interaction occurs. Thus, we can more specifically say that human agency vis-à-vis the computer takes place at the fulcrum of its two realities: a computer is both an ongoing computational process (literally voltage flows, but also the programs that are constantly running) and a series of discrete states (i.e., the window and icon metaphors, but also the translation of voltage flows into changes in voltage tracked through ones and zeros). To use a computer, then, is to map these two incommensurable realities into the impossible incommunicative totality that we call a "computer," a mapping that is achieved by spatializing temporal vectors.

It is not surprising, then, that digital sound is conventionally overdetermined by its visual components. For example, one can sensibly speak of moving samples around and, moreover, anyone who has taught such programs will likely have received student works constructed around the appearance of the waveforms (e.g., through visual symmetry, or the appearance of a narrative arc through the addition and subtraction of active tracks). *Exurbia* contrasts this tendency not by eradicating visuality through a dark interface (which would, in any case, not eradicate visuality at all but merely expand its purview à la Cage's positivization of silence), but instead by using visuality to instigate the types of temporal processes that are constitutive of sound in analog settings. Users click, drag, and even type numbers in the *Exurbia* interface, but the effects of their actions—in the sample, the composition, and in the networked community—are only registered aurally.[46]

One result of this temporalized interface is that individual opportunities to edit in *Exurbia* literally go by in an instant, since they take place in real time. Editing, then, becomes less a process of cutting and pasting and shifts instead toward channeling and remixing, metaphors that promote the constitutive entanglement of the edited sound, the obscured technical and social relations of the platform, and the act of listening/editing. Moreover, this phenomenon is heightened by the exclusive use of destructive editing, which again works to resist the reversibility of signs that visual editing programs assume, and that visuality in general institutes in its spatializing capacity.[47]

Indeed, sound in general tends to be resistant to being represented as data in at least two ways.[48] First, it is differentially and temporally embodied in that, as Aden Evens points out, "to hear is to experience air pressure changing. . . . One does not hear air pressure, but one hears it change over time [such that] to hear a pitch that does not change is to hear as constant something that is nothing but change."[49] Put simply, this means that "to hear is to hear difference," a quality that is not captured in the positivist framework of data but that is activated in *Exurbia*'s editing procedures.[50] Indeed, when returning to the program, one can only listen for other users' interventions by listening for differences that are not verifiable.

A second way in which sound resists being expressed as data is through being relational, in the sense that it resists being placed: sound is never quite where it purports to be. For example, in contrast to a beam of light panning across a screen, a recorded sound is spatialized via a relative difference in intensity between two polarized loudspeakers: if it is perceived to be 80 percent to the right, this speaks to the fact that the right loudspeaker is four times as intense as the left. The twist that makes sound relational rather than simply relative—and which extends this element even to monophonic sounds—is that the sound also isn't where it appears to be (i.e., coming from the loudspeaker[s]) since it only comes to be as a sound through the differential act of hearing discussed above, which is the very act that would place it where it isn't. That is, the sense that the sound is coming from the loudspeaker is created by the material conjunction of that sound and the listener's auditory system (usually and most prominently their ears, though never entirely); since this touching is only (paradoxically) made possible by a (systemic) separation between the source and its reception, it is not really sensible to speak of the sound as originating in the source.[51] In the case of *Exurbia*, then, this is emphasized through the impossibility of composing in isolation from other users' interventions, even though all editing is performed within the fiction of such isolation.

In both these cases, a key factor is *Exurbia*'s emphasis on real time, which acts in the program through an aesthetics of speed and dissipation. That is, the realness of *Exurbia*'s editing is articulated through the perpetual vanishing of the present through a constant evaporation of the sound object—the fiction of a sample that exists as a sound outside of its sounding articulation—that takes place precisely through its incommunicative (aural) appearance. And yet the opposite is also true in that the cumulative effect of this approach is a painfully slow experience of digital music composition. According to anecdotes from users, pieces take roughly forty to fifty times as long to create as they would in a standard waveform editor. Whereas with the latter, for example, one might make any number of edits to a recording prior to even listening to it, in *Exurbia* each of these takes the full time of the sample and/or the piece into which the sample is being inserted.[52] Here again, then, this slowness in editing amounts to a qualitative difference independent of the different compositional decisions that flow from it, because it temporalizes a process that is regularly thought spatially (indeed, even the term *sound file* suggests atemporality).[53]

If important elements of *Exurbia*'s intervention can be captured under the sign of temporality, this by no means exhausts its incommunicative world building. We can additionally note that exclusively registering edits aurally means that they are held mnemonically in a different manner than in a waveform editor; insofar as users are composing pieces, these pieces are made of markedly different matter than is typically the case. There is first the dramatic vulnerability of each piece to every other—due to their use of a shared set of samples that is constantly changing in ways that are difficult to control—the result of which is a constitutive and unavoidable impermanence. More interesting, though, is the way that this forces participants to internalize their compositions in an unconventional manner. Unlike improvisational contexts that feature similar levels of contingency and ephemerality, *Exurbia*'s compositional orientation demands that one remember one's piece as an entire piece since the only way to know if there have been changes since one was last in the environment is to remember what it sounded like when one last left it: edited samples are inserted into a master track, so that the implicit injunction is to remember the piece as one has composed it, to provisionally bracket out the contingencies built into the system, or to at least conceptualize them as something that happens to the composition rather than as something that is integral to it.

Combined with the slowness of working in the *Exurbia* environment, this emphasis on memory in its unverifiable aspect creates a sense of intimacy with the work by giving the impression of a greater portion of the piece being "stored" directly in one's memory. Here again, the cultural dominance of visuality is pushed against itself: we are so accustomed to using visual abstractions—textual, iconic, and so on—as mnemonic devices that their absence gives us the sense of a more embodied experience. Thus, for example, we typically have the sensation of conscious cognition somehow taking place independently of the actual workings of our bodies, in contrast to which nonconscious forms of memory—commonly called muscle memory—are often constructed as the self to which we should be true in our decision making. The speciousness of this claim in no way undermines its effects, and indeed it is no less beguiling when, for example, an individual with advanced Alzheimer's can still sing a childhood song while accompanying themselves on the piano. It is precisely this alibi of a mind-body separation—integral to so many quotidian activities, despite its having been thoroughly critiqued for the past several decades—that generates intimacy in *Exurbia*. I might go so far as to suggest that participants in *Exurbia* have the opportunity to know their compositions in a deeper affective register, in the same sense that an earworm can be said to crawl more deeply into our psyches than a memory of a visual image because it is persistent and involuntary.[54] Accepting that any ascription of agency is predicated on a (necessary) fiction, we might say that the conventional fiction of using the computer is supplemented in *Exurbia* by one of the computer aurally investing us with our compositions. This is a fully dataphasic relation, then, wherein that which the computer receives (i.e., the singular dynamism of affective processes) and that which we cannot (i.e., that of our actions that do not come from any part of ourselves that we can know) persist precisely because their failure to communicate nonetheless incommunicates.

It is worth underscoring that the coarseness, slowness, and embodied internalization I've described work against the logic of info-capitalism that privileges efficiency, optimization, and atomization. In this, *Exurbia* aligns with what Katherine Behar calls "decelerationist aesthetics": the piece impedes speed and immediacy by "taking back and taking up space and time," rejecting the contemporary privileging of atomistic, liberal human subjectivity.[55] As such, there is a culturally subversive component to *Exurbia* that reappropriates information (via sound) incommunicatively.

This is particularly evident in the way that *Exurbia* enacts community. In the same way that *Exurbia* pressures the metaphorical dominance of vision in computational sonic interfaces, it also leverages numerous assumptions about the nature of community as one component of the immaterial origin of online social behaviors. Importantly, one should note that sociality is not a contemporary add-on to the computer (i.e., coming to be with the advent of social networking sites like Facebook) but a crucial component of its history. As Alexis Madrigal argues, with social networking sites, "We're not giving our personal data in exchange for the ability to share links with friends. Massive numbers of people already did that outside the social networks. Rather, we're exchanging our personal data in exchange for the ability to publish and archive a record of our sharing," in part because the knowledge of having successfully shared is as important as the sharing itself.[56] This raises the question: to what extent are the communities that spring up as both the cause and effect of this sense of sharing specifically dependent on a record created in alignment with the dominant tropes of computational visuality?

Exurbia gestures toward this question by making the strange, aurally modulated individual compositional experience that it offers contingent on and in important senses secondary to the behaviors of an online community.[57] On one hand, *Exurbia*'s communal experience is characterized by a vulnerability to others that recalls, say, a multiuser online game: one invests a significant amount of time and energy creating an avatar—in this case a composition—that is from the outset oriented both internally and externally. That is, the avatar acts as a kind of manipulable virtual mirror through which one amplifies and attenuates certain features of oneself, while at the same time acting as a screen through which one negotiates a social community. Vulnerability, then, emerges in part from the recursive discrepancies between these two identities—between the signifying ecologies of the mirror and screen—which catalyze activity in one another without being able to cause it: the coexcitations are incommunicative insofar as they simply enact the constraints and affordances of the system that is perturbed (in addition to doing something else that can't quite be pinned down). *Exurbia* engages this paradigm, but pushes its incommunicative vectors further because its vulnerability doesn't necessarily coincide with any acknowledgment of one's impact on others. That is, at every level of the program, visual and textual cues of others' actions and desires are absent. Unlike most online community art projects, there are no chat forums, comment boxes, or even counters. There is, in short, no way to collectively narrate the connections between communal flows, pulsations, and mutations and the individuals who instigate them. The ethical worlds of each individual and the community are seemingly isolated from one another: the community acts on the participant by interfering with their relatively intimate compositional process, but the participant is able to choose whether or not they will be aware of or even acknowledge their own impact vis-à-vis the larger community. That is, the link between digitally networked activities and online communities is denaturalized: unlike most digital settings, where the community is the necessary and a priori stage for articulations of individuality, participants have to actually choose to seek out the ramifications of their actions for other individuals in *Exurbia*. A paradoxical incommunicative truism thus comes to light: it is only in a setting where it is impossible to verify the ramifications of one's actions (and where it is by no means necessary to attempt to do so consciously) that the priority of the relationality of those actions can robustly be avowed.

In beta testing, there was little evidence that such considerations played an active role (an exception being instances of "griefing"), which raises questions about the relation between sound and online communities.[58] *Exurbia*, for example, might be considered a means of testing whether a predominantly aural environment can provide sufficient ground for users to develop a sensibility and/or ethics with respect to other members of a digital community. If so, what changes in this configuration, and how can we begin to listen to these voices? If not, how might this help us unpack the complex considerations that are built into the word *community* as it obtains online? While it is a cliché that internet technologies have the potential to both kill and cultivate communities, *Exurbia* realigns this problematic to suggest ways in which internet communities are conventionally constituted through an exaggerated visuality, specifically through vision's spatializing capacity. What this points to—borrowing from Rosalind Krauss—is the expanded field of online community, the way that the discourse of community takes part in the materiality of digital networks.

Answering the question of whether this goes both ways is beyond the scope of this chapter, but it is certainly worth asking: to what extent does living in the afterlife of data—where the discourse of digitality is capable of working independently of any actual technologies—inform our offline understanding of community? In this light, it is worth pointing out that the sort of community that *Exurbia* promotes would be difficult to monetize, and that this at least suggests the possibility that the visuality and archivality that seem natural or obvious in most computer interfaces are as much a product of a predatory logic of commodification as they are a matter of code, design, functionality, and such. What an analysis of *Exurbia* also seems to reveal, then, is how much both the online and offline community of the digital networked world is thoroughly capitalistic. Working this revelation through specifically aural incommunication doesn't exactly open an alternative network model/operation, but does sound a certain nascent indeterminacy that is smuggled within the seeming fatality of technics.[59]

In this, *Exurbia*'s relation to digitally networked communities aligns with a general tendency of sound to be semiotically parasitic: sound tends to be implicated in other systems and rhetorics of meaning (such as music and language) but is not itself meaningful, except through the recursions that it introduces into these systems. Put differently, sound tends to intensify; we can note, for example, that better-quality audio in audiovisual pre-

42 Chapter One

sentations encourages viewers to perceive visual displays as having higher resolution, while the opposite is not true.[60] In the case of *Exurbia*, then, the compositions become avatars by virtue of the digitally networked community, but in so doing desublimate the visual orientation of "avatar" as a locus of material semiotics.

If the very nature of online communities is thus tied to a specific medial expression, this suggests that mediality constitutes a potential site for political activity even (and especially!) as it remains incommunicable. Beyond the specific challenges that it raises, then, *Exurbia* demonstrates the broader potential of thinking the problem of medium specificity through specific practices, putting the medium specificities of sound and digital technologies into play in a way that emphasizes their operational rather than categorical dimensions. In this, a sonic pragmatism is not only produced but specifically produced in the context of that which it affects and which affects it—once and for all, but also again and again.

In the context of a chapter about medium specificity in music and sound art, *Exurbia* thus demonstrates the incommunicative dimension of medium specificity as that which both undermines any constative ontological claims about sound and reinforces such claims' impacts. If we are to speak in a specific and historically informed way about art, technology, and culture, it is necessary to keep the imbrication of materiality and discourse at the front of our minds. Doing so does not consist in bracketing out discourse, it also must move beyond the implicit tautology of saying that everything is discourse as though this means something concrete and limited rather than being the means through which experience takes hold as such in order to also be the more-thans of other trajectories altogether.

Networking Sound and Medium Specificity   43

2

Listening and Technicity

The concept is never borne of an individual. Concepts are gathered in the sociality of existence. . . . Concepts are made in the activation of the ecology they gather forth.

ERIN MANNING, "FUGITIVELY, APPROXIMATELY"

Sometimes I hear in one ear what I should, by all rights, hear in the other. It is an unsettling experience, because stereo inversion isn't nearly as consistent a phenomenon as one would expect from its technical iteration: put your earphones on backward and the signals are inverted, but it turns out very little of one's listening biome has anything to do with this technical profile of signaletics. Between my ears there is interposed something that is animated by more incommunicative forces that one can only hear to hear.

So really, I should say that I hear in each ear how I should hear in the other, since stereophonic listening is rarely a question of what one hears: a finger snapped next to my right ear is audible in both, but differently so. The "whats" in question aren't the objects that are heard, but rather the spacings that are dynamically crafted by the always particular and ongoing "hows" of intercochlear (in) communication. *Rightness* and *leftness* describe textural possibilities of the dynamic relations that listening at once is and affords: they describe feelings as much as places, which is why—if one bends one's circuits just so—rightness can migrate to leftness without losing what it is. Sometimes I hear in one ear what I should, by all rights, hear in the other.

One might say: experiential qualia incommunicate in and as the spatialization of their immanent differentiation. This is obscure in theory, but blessedly simple in practice. Such became clear to me a couple years ago when I beta-tested a work in progress by the artist Jessica Thompson, which involved attaching microphones to my shoes and routing their audio signals in real time to earphones that I was wearing.[1] Effectively, this created a situation wherein I listened through my feet.[2] What I realized is that on one hand one's environment is reconfigured in really interesting ways when one listens through one's feet: the texture of the ground, for example, becomes a central determinant in what one hears, as well as in the horizon of one's hearing. Standing in the middle of a street, one can hear the rumble of approaching automobiles from quite some distance but much less distinctly the voices of pedestrians passing by more closely on the sidewalk. Likewise, standing in tall grass prevents one from hearing much of anything besides the rubbing of said grass on one's feet. On the other hand, while all of the above is true it is also the case that the experience of listening through one's feet is so wonderful precisely because one's ears are also not on the ground. That is, the pleasure lies precisely in the doubling of one's senses; the pleasure lies in feeling how one's ears are in two places at once.[3]

Such doubling is a classic aesthetic strategy and indeed one that has taken on increased prominence in the context of mixed reality technologies and, more recently, current wearable virtual reality technologies. I had an experience of this a few years ago when I saw the film *Gravity* in a movie theater equipped with motorized chairs that move in sync with the sounds and images of the film. In *Gravity*, the most remarkable impact of this technical apparatus was when the protagonist (played by Sandra Bullock) was floating through outer space, with my seat moving synchronously in a way that emphasized the spherical reality of zero gravity. The experience was remarkable in and of itself, but for me it worked against the experience of the film as a narrative because it interrupted the "out of body-ness" through which narrative films become immersive. As James Lastra and others have noted, for most images on a screen, "scale and angle are functions of *narrative* emphasis [rather than] precise perception."[4] There is typically a bodily experience of disembodiment that happens when one is taken up in the experience of something like a novel or film, which is why we can speak of "losing ourselves" in these experiences. Since this disembodiment is still an experience of embodiment, we might say that the motorized chair works to double one's bodily experience in a way that, ironically, makes its immersive responsiveness lead to a diminished sense of immersion. One is aware of one's body in the cinema, and this makes it difficult to give oneself to the (embodied) disembodiment through which a narrative proceeds. Sometimes more is less. The motorized chair crafted my body as a site of doubling, but was anathema to the character identifications, problem-solving challenges, visual and sonic expansions, and so on, that are the characteristic doublings through which Hollywood films typically work as narratives. There was an incoherence to my experience of myself with myself that stemmed from the qualitative differences between the bodily doublings of the seat and the bodily doublings of the narrative.

Chapter 1 approached sound in its incommunicative dimension, specifically demonstrating how a particular concatenation of sound and digital network technology affords novel experiences of their incommunicative coimplication. In this chapter, I extend my engagement with sound to the phenomenon of listening. Why listening? Because listening most readily affords the kind of active receptivity that a dataphasic disposition demands: the metaphors of listening align at once with the propensity for being sensitive to the thoughts that want to work their way through one and the ways that such thoughts are themselves spuriously epistemic, in Robin James's (critical) sense.[5] As I discuss in the final chapter of this book, there is something of a compulsion in listening that affords a distributed understanding of agency, even if (still following James) such distributions are not necessarily indicative of a departure from the governing logics of contemporary neoliberalism.

With this in mind, in what follows I do not so much ask what listening is, but rather think through what it would mean to listen differently: what are the latches and levers of listening, and how are these latched and leveraged? How can practices of listening otherwise agitate the contradictory notions of agency that are at work in the (computational) appearance of universal exchangeability that is so seductive today? In this approach, we can acknowledge the technicity that obtains in listening, whether a computer is involved or not. This, in turn, can help us think about not just the points of contact between humans and computers with respect to listening, but more importantly about the modulative coconstitution of listening and computation on the grounds of technicity that constitutes another of their incommunicative tendencies.

Thankfully, some things are easier done than said, and just as a discussion of the artwork *Exurbia* anchored my argument in chapter 1, this chapter works through another tangible artifact. However, whereas chapter 1 emphasized what *Exurbia* does as a completed artwork, in this chapter I discuss the process of working on an art-adjacent project (called Fathead), the orientation of which has changed dramatically over the several years I've developed it. As with a certain portion of my work, Fathead has involved building some tangible devices that help me not only focus on certain specific questions and problems but also attend to how those questions and problems change in being pursued pragmatically. Incommunications play themselves materially and conceptually when pursued pragmatically, and that often means that unexamined assumptions and conventions are sounded out. As a result, the discussed changes are as indicative of certain sorts of audible incommunications as that which results from them.

Fathead began as a wearable interface that alters the scale of the wearer's auditory *Umwelt*.[6] In quotidian experience, the short temporal delay and amplitude diminution that are experienced when a sound travels from one side of one's head to the other plays a prominent role in how we spatialize that sound. That is, a sound that comes directly from the left side of one's head will arrive at one's right ear approximately 1/1,000th of a second after it arrives at the left ear and will be ever so slightly diminished in volume to a degree described by the inverse square law.[7] The first Fathead prototypes amplified these differences (in various ways, as I will discuss) to simulate how the world could sound if one's head were instead one thousand feet wide, a width that was chosen because at sea level, on a clear day, sound travels at approximately one thousand feet per second.[8] Thus, an auditor wearing Fathead listening to a sound that came directly from their left would hear it at a diminished volume in their right ear a full second after hearing it in their left ear (figure 2.1).

The initial device itself (and many of the myriad prototypes that followed) basically consisted of two small microphones, a pocket-sized computing device (such as a smartphone, or in some instances a Raspberry Pi[9]), and a (preferably noise-canceling) set of headphones. One microphone is

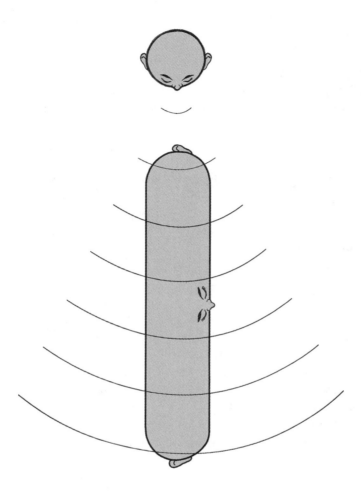

Fig. 2.1. Fathead audio delay. Illustration by Luke Painter.

physically attached to each earpiece of the headphones, with the wearable computer acting as an intermediary in the flow of the signal from the microphones to the headphones. There are a number of different ways that I computed the simulation, but with this basic setup they all amounted to adding delay to and diminishing the amplitude of each of the stereo signals in proportion to the direction of the auditor's head (or, really, their ears). As a result, what one gets with the most basic iteration of Fathead is a situation where the microdifferences in delay and volume that imperceptibly shape quotidian listening are amplified into conscious awareness. As I hope is clear from the discussion in chapter 1, this quantitative amplification constitutes a qualitative change; indeed, one of the conceptual gambits of incommunication is that all quantitative changes can be experienced in the particularity of their qualitative shifts.[10]

Naturally, this amplification into conscious awareness makes elements of the experience accessible to experimentation, the most simple of which involved rotating my head on its horizontal axis. The ability to rotate my head 180 degrees in significantly less than one second means that I can theoretically impact the order of words being spoken if I listen from just one ear. Likewise, I can theoretically use such turning motions as volume faders for each ear.

While these experiments are interesting, in practice by far the most pronounced consequence of having this sort of thousand-foot-wide head is the extreme Doppler shifts. A Doppler shift is the effect of a sliding pitch that one hears when, for example, a vehicle drives by with its siren on; the "whoosh" of any passing car evidences the same phenomenon. This glissando is, basically, created by sound waves piling up on one another: in the classic example of an approaching siren, for instance, the emergency vehicle is emitting a frequency at a fixed rate at the source, but the waves don't arrive at a fixed frequency to the listener because the distance they have to travel decreases as the vehicle approaches. The motion at the source thus redounds to increase the frequency as the vehicle approaches, and since perceived pitch is a function of frequency, this results in a higher pitch at the point of reception than that which was emitted. The frequency then decreases as the vehicle recedes, thereby lowering the perceived pitch. In the case of the Fathead prototype, the same principle obtains, but rather than the motion occurring at the point of origin, it happens at the points of reception (figure 2.2). The plural here is interesting because a single signal is

Listening and Technicity   49

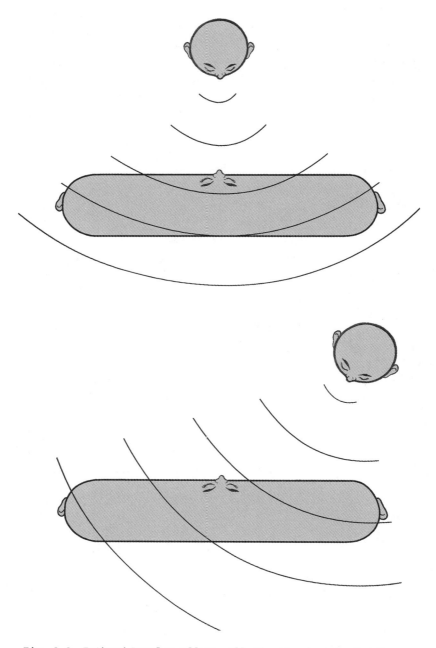

Fig. 2.2. Fathead Doppler effect. Illustration by Luke Painter.

split into its stereophonic reception, with the motion of each channel (i.e., each ear) effecting a Doppler shift in the opposite direction of the other. Though the resulting shifts are inversely symmetrical (like a teeter-totter), they don't offset in their perception, so there is a strange experience of one's stereo field being sutured and sundered in the same gesture.

Because of the extreme scaling involved in Fathead's simulation, simply turning one's head from left to right has the (imaginary, but no less real) aural impact of each ear having moved five hundred feet, so that even relatively small movements produce pronounced Doppler effects. This is pleasant in and of itself, but more fascinating is that the prominence of these effects aggregates as a general impression that the pitch of things is much less fixed than we typically perceive it to be: any sounds with even vaguely discernible pitches (which includes many sounds) are unmoored, variously drifting, slithering, and vaulting toward and away from their decreasingly discernible original pitch. That is, the Doppler is interesting because one feels as though the pitch center of one's world is both moving and pluralizing, a sensation that is made even stranger by the fact that when the Doppler effect stops, the pitch centers don't so much move back as settle and reaggregate. This is a kind of sessile modulation of what is being heard: if one is listening with Fathead to a piece of music, the piece doesn't modulate from key to key but instead crafts a kind of nonmodulating vitality within each key. Fathead crafts an intramodulatory vector within that which one hears, tuning in to the intras of incommunications.

One can listen to sample recordings made with Fathead online (preferably through headphones), but the effect is greatly reduced.[11] This is the case because the haptic relationship between one's movements and what one hears is missing—or, really, recast—in any recording, but also (specific to Fathead) because there is a haptic asynchrony that comes about with listening with a thousand-foot-wide head: a sound directly in front of one takes approximately a half second to reach each ear—a half-second delay is just a fact of life when your head is a thousand feet wide.[12] Wearing Fathead doesn't quite make *the* missing half second perceptible, but it makes *a* missing half second perceptible in and as a transductive, spatializing echo that is crafted between sight and sound.

In a sense, the qualitative dimension of delay is brought out in Fathead, supplementing its measurable character. The delay is often unsettling, catalyzing a feeling of being at once acutely present and strangely distant. Present, because one buzzes with a new configuration of one's senses, one's eyes scrambling for a purchase that would let them skip the beat that insists on separating them from what is heard. One is strangely present, too, because there are weird congruencies of timing when what one hears does seem to line up with what is seen, a temporal coincidence that isn't really that surprising given both the world of "continuous multiscalar transition" that we live in and the spaces of inscription in which Fathead is worn (e.g., musical listening scenarios, conversations); taken together, these increase the "probability of capturing instances of differential repetition" and therefore also the discovery of coincidences.[13]

And yet there is also a certain self-dissociation that comes with hearing everything in delay: what is experienced temporally as a deferral is also experienced spatially as a gap within oneself that is widened by the heightened reflexivity of hearing oneself seeing. That is, to the extent that one's senses can be categorically differentiated from one another—which is limited, but not altogether nonexistent—the temporally noncoincident experience of watching something a half second ahead of what one hears is parsed as a temporally continuous experience of bodily noncoincidence: analogously to the narrative experience of embodied disembodiment, one hears that what one is hearing has somehow lagged behind one's vision without ever ceasing to hear and see. The intersensory echo at once hollows one's body (through its transductive spatialization) and enunciates this incommunicative internality as the dynamic embodiment of which a body is the product.

In this sense, the delay feels specifically technical; it feels connected to the autonomic technics that are always involved in listening (and perception in general). That is, what is audible in the delay is—among other things—precisely the machinations of perception, the "'originary' coupling of the human and the technical" that grounds experience as such and that "can only be known through its effects."[14] Thus, this feels weird not because it isn't natural and not even because this technical element is explicitly sensible, but rather because the ongoingness of this coupling—the coactivity of the mutual inclusion—is somehow both conscious and nonconscious. The autonomic technics of the delay crafts an incommunicative continuity wherein conscious and nonconscious thinking are not experientially opposed to one another. Put differently, the techniques of embodiment are aestheticized in and as the delay: there is something technically aesthetic—something quasi-technical that is embodied but remains outside of the techniques of embodiment—that is activated.[15]

While the experiences that Fathead affords are remarkable, the processes involved in making the various versions of it are more germane to the question of incommunication and, ultimately, that of how one might listen to computers incommunicatively.[16] To that end, the prehistory of the project is worth noting: like a lot of my work, Fathead grew from an initial idea that was mistaken—taken in error, but taken nonetheless. Quite simply, I read one day—on one of the many (possibly spurious) lay scientific websites that proliferate on the web—about the way that certain species of Arctic owl have an acute vertical stereophonic sense that they take advantage of in hunting. Specifically, the story suggested that some owls hunt small prey (such as rodents) that scurry along on top of frozen ground that is underneath a thick layer of soft snow. Using a vertical stereophonic acuity similar to human horizontal accuracy, the owls are able to dynamically track the location of the rodents despite their not being visible (since they are under the snow and being tracked from above). When the owl strikes, it swoops downward with sufficient speed to blast through the snow, snatches the rodent in its beak, and pulls up at precisely the right moment to avoid smashing its beak on the hard, frozen earth. In short, the owl listens past the visible surface—which is something that sound affords, since density and resonance correlate—and is able to track the rodent three-dimensionally without actually seeing it. In the species of owl in question, their ability to discern vertically—and the specific form of depth perception at which they excel—comes about in part because each of their ears are at slightly different heights on their head, thus creating the kind of microdifferences (discussed above) that Fathead amplifies. (Again, other factors also contribute to this ability, and indeed—as will become clear—perceptual capacities can never be entirely derived from purely mechanical processes.)

Compared to owls, humans have a dramatically impoverished sense of vertical stereo. While many humans have remarkably accurate horizontal stereo perception (such that, for example, it is relatively easy to hear in which direction the page of a book is being turned), this is simply not the case vertically. As a result, human aural depth perception likewise pales in comparison to that of the owls in question, since aural depth perception is a function of the concatenation of horizontal and vertical percepts.[17] So in reading about these owls, the mistaken thought that I had was to wonder how I could simulate that kind of vertical auditory perception for myself. The mistake of that thought, of course, lies in it bespeaking precisely the nonrelational thinking that this book is contesting. One can't simply abstract and reassign a single component of a complex system like a listening body; as much is clear from Maturana et al.'s work demonstrating that a "frog's visual system does not so much represent reality as *construct* it," from Uexküll's canonical work on animal worlds, Bateson's work on affordance, and from any degree of patient reflection.[18] To describe an owl's listening as human listening with supplementary vertical stereo capacities would be like characterizing Google's data collection as just a library with a larger and faster card catalog. Instead, differences produce differences and are themselves products of differences, such that they can't simply be extracted. When we change one thing, everything changes. If my mistake failed to take this into account, then, I was recruited into this mistake by the nonrelationality of the Regime of Computation in which I live, which spun its thoughts—its incommunications—through me despite my explicitly not believing them.[19]

To return to the owl anecdote, what I realized in reflecting on my mistaken, habituated inclination to simulate the vertical stereophony of the owl's hearing was that each of the particular ways that my impulse was naively incommunicated; they each pointed to different specific and contingent sites of such doublings. Any simulation was always going to fail at a global level, but the specific ways that the total systemic integrity would fall apart as a gestalt simulation would each reveal something of an infolding of scales and relations of perception.[20] One could even go so far as to say that such infoldings are actually what constitute any experience of embodiment, because all bodies are incoherently multiscalar. The scalar entanglements that constitute a body are intra-incommunicative, in part because the notion of scale involved in correlating distinct bodily activities works precisely through the logic of exchange that it disproves in its singular plurality. *Morphology* is always plural, and indeed always more plural than it seems.

In any case, it was when I latched onto this understanding that simulational failures indicated sites of systemically incoherent perceptual entanglements that I decided to simplify the Fathead apparatus so as to leverage their actual specificity. Rather than pursuing the project of introducing a vertical stereo field to my listening, I decided to start by playing with my existing stereo field in ways that would bring me directly in contact with the systemic incoherencies that are inevitable in the simulative paradigm.

As is typically the case when working with computers, the notion of play at work in the choices I made in building Fathead prototypes related to exploiting the ways that its constituent systems work rather than making them work in new ways per se. In a cultural moment when most computer programs have recycled so much code from other programs such that "no living person understands the programs in their totality," the exploitative method that used to characterize hacking has become the coding norm.[21] The inevitable incoherencies that come with Fathead's scalar simulations necessitated interventions, so that the decisions I made were always in response to such limitations: a system is a system only insofar as it is delimited as such, so a system in a world will always both limit and exploit itself. At a design level, this means that the components of Fathead—mapped in this case as the device, the wearer of the device, and the dynamic environments that are called forth in and as both the site and product of those components' interactions—can connect to one another because they in some sense remain distinct. This further means that one can intervene in the relational experience as a whole by leveraging the internal operations of the components. Indeed, this is why I've made reference to various iterations of Fathead, namely because part of what I initially wanted to experiment with was the indeterminacy of these part-whole relationships: by intensifying the affordances particular to individual components of Fathead, I was able to reconfigure the experience as whole.

A few examples will help illustrate. In one iteration, I leveraged the tremendous dynamism that is involved in the psychoacoustic element of listening in order to better experience the interear effects of the delays and concomitant Doppler shifts. In that case, I significantly downgraded the degree of volume decay that would take place over the computed distances, knowing that the simulated changes in distance could still be perceived based on combinations of other factors. Put simply, there is more involved in aural depth perception than just changes in volume, just as there is more involved in visual depth perception than changes in size: a greyhound doesn't become a dachshund when it moves further away. As a result, the actual volume decay in the Fathead doesn't have to be realistic in order to be perceived as such, and, indeed, diminishing this decay makes the experience more realistic in some respects (just as, for example, the constraints of a film set can in some senses result in a more realistic effect than a Dogme 95 film). In short, this iteration of Fathead leverages a psychoacoustic ability to imagine past existing scalar incoherencies, intensifying that ability to stretch the coherent experience that is "feeling realistic" to include the impossible reality of a thousand-foot-wide head.[22]

I experimented with the opposite approach in a different iteration, sustaining the expected degree of volume decay. Interestingly, this approach not only significantly limits the range of audibility (as expected), but also retextures a certain psychoacoustic incommunication: with the extreme changes in volume comes the sense of one's ears being decoupled from one another such that the sensation is of hearing two discrete informatic channels rather than a stereo field. That is, the actuality of the spatial expansion—expressed through the inverse square law of volume diminution—stresses the structural integrity of one's typical relational hearing to a point where it splits into a different sort of system, not unlike the way that one's aural attention is reconfigured by speaking on a telephone held to one ear.

The above two examples each execute a virtual scalar expansion after the moment of reception, in effect scaling everything that one hears upward to the same extent. Entirely different approaches are also possible, including (for example) the use of radio transmitters situated five hundred feet away in each direction from the auditor's head so that there is (in many settings) no correlation between what is being seen and what is being heard. In that case, the quality of experience changes from an expansion of the auditor from within to an expansion into a figuration of virtuality that has become familiar with telepresence technologies. Perhaps more interestingly, the primary technical challenge of computing the simulation shifts from one that is executed by a scaling algorithm to one that is coordinated through the movements of several actors, redistributing the auditor's agencies in challenging (if coarsely executed) ways.

Again, each different version of Fathead works by working a particular set of perceptual doublings, which doublings only exist as such insofar as they invaginate incongruent sensory realities. And indeed, the notion of experience that underwrites these realities is not that of an autonomous subject, but rather of "aggregates of multiple and heterogeneous, overlapping agencies complexly imbricated with the total situation or environment at [a] given moment of occurrence."[23] Following recent scholarship that springs from a reinvigorated interest in Alfred North Whitehead, such aggregates need not be (and are not always) routed through human beings: experience is not the privileged terrain of higher-order consciousness but is instead the causal efficacy through which worlds world. As such, Fathead doesn't infold only the relational entanglements of my and the device's listening techniques, but also something of the logic of that to which I wanted to listen. Put simply, that to which one listens has logics of its own that afford and constrain relational configurations.

For instance, in the initial approaches to Fathead, my emphasis was on crafting a device that I could use in classical music concert halls to listen to concert music. Beyond its avian provenance, Fathead was part of a series of self-interventions I explored in a period of my life during which I'd often find myself in such settings with an interest in hearing a particular (usually contemporary) piece, but having to sit through canonical common practice period pieces to get to that part of the program. (My interest in Beethoven was substantially reinvigorated by listening to his work with a thousand-foot-wide head.) As a result, for Fathead to work, it had to sustain, to at least a limited extent, the particular kind of hallucination that we call music; that is, it had to craft a plane that allows for the coexistent incommunication of the device's scaling machinations, my bodily listening system's processual ones, and the sense of a piece of music existing as a distinct entity with a structural integrity based in part on the surface tension of its sounds.

Put differently (and as I outlined in chapter 1), concert music has its own intra-incommunicative networks that infold in and as the doublings that it is. The perceptual doublings I chose to intensify, then, were chosen in part in order to be able to hear the perceptual doublings—the multiscalar incoherencies—that take shape in and as concert music. In this sense, Fathead became a way of taking the technical elements of music seriously by not just listening to pitches and rhythms, but also listening to the various entrainments that are knotted together with pitch and rhythm in and as musical incommunication within it, in its extramusical contact with the world, and especially in its particular texturing of (the [un]sustainability of) that binary.

Listening and Technicity   57

These first iterations of Fathead were all completed a few years prior to this writing, and I was generally fairly happy with the kinds of things I was learning. I've certainly had lots of fun with my thousand-foot-wide heads. But then one day I heard a story about a seemingly unrelated study—the veracity of which I've never confirmed—that shifted my perspective significantly. The study suggested that there is a propensity for pedestrians speaking on mobile phones to be struck by vehicles not because they walk into traffic per se, but because they escape the driver's visual field by talking on the phone. That is, this class of accident happens because the pedestrian fails to share the customary, nonconscious affective cues of recognition with the driver such that their particular vitality disappears into the driver's traffic environment. The communicative tool—the mobile phone— works perfectly, and the pedestrian disappears into its working . . . only to arrive incommunicatively on the hood of an oncoming vehicle.

I've thought about this a lot since first hearing about it, and I won't repeat much of what I've written elsewhere.[24] But the lesson of the study that skewed my approach to Fathead lay in its suggestion of an incoherence— scalar and modular—between its individual prosthetic relations and a kind of relationality in which a prosthetic understanding is secondary. Insofar as I was thinking of Fathead prosthetically, I was learning about the perceptual doublings of what Anna Munster calls "informatic affect" at the level of an individual, wherein an individual feels "the difference between being in the body and representing/mapping the body from the outside" in "a process of subjective bodily recomposition that occurs in relation to the alterity that pattern and code renderings open up for us."[25] However, what the pedestrian–mobile phone example suggests is less an individual perceptual doubling and more a worldly experiential one. That is, the pedestrian's disappearance is not really a single movement into a tool, but rather the revelation of a distributive ecology composed of enmeshed material conditions that can't be collapsed into a closed system: the persistent worldly incoherence that unfolds in and as incommunication. It's true: the pedestrian goes away, disappearing into the mobile phone's global systematicity. However, it is also the case that the pedestrian arrives at their telelocation(s), at the postglobal technical ecology of cellular, satellite, and smartphone technologies that both exists in its own right and textures contemporary sociality. The pedestrian appears, then, but differently and distributedly in a way

58   Chapter Two

that discloses an incommunicative circuit through which incommensurable realities relate even as they remain discrete.

And so, Fathead has become (in collaboration with brilliant students at several universities) a project that aims to think through broader, relational understandings of human-technology ecologies in their incommunicative profile. To this end, I am now more inclined to build prototypes that are designed for seminar settings: in gathering for such seminars with students and colleagues, we each wear different listening prosthetics (including, often, a Fathead for me), but the interesting part is that we do so while reading and discussing a selection of texts.[26] Often, the individual reading of the texts too is undertaken while wearing prosthetics, and I have also experimented with numerous different setups and durations for the meetings. In this approach, the emphasis of the project shifts toward an engagement with how different morphologies impact simple practices of knowledge sharing (e.g., reading, reflecting on, and discussing a text). That is, I've begun to explore how a change in scale of individual hearing affects collective knowledge in its relational dimension, and to flesh out various ways to palpate the incoherencies between the individual systems at work in those relations.

In doing so, another genealogy of Fathead has emerged, complementing both the prosthetic story of the owl and the media-ecological insight gleaned from the pedestrian–mobile phone accident. I'd forgotten that in November 2015, Anna Munster described (and to an extent demonstrated) a related experience during a plenary address to a conference I co-organized, Tuning Speculation III.[27] In a research-creation project led by Erin Manning called Immediations: Art, Media, Event, participants aiming to cultivate techniques for "collaborative thinking-making-feeling" have developed Skype reading groups. As Munster describes:

> Setting a difficult and often complex philosophical or scientific text ahead of time, we meet every couple of weeks in online audio mode only using the Skype platform in order to preserve bandwidth but allow for as many people as possible to contribute. The sessions are full of technical "failures": breakdowns in transmission, signal feedback, network glitches not to mention the ambient noise of people forgetting to mute their microphones when their dog rabidly barks in the background. And yet we have persevered because all this signaletic matter

that takes place through the Skype platform together with all the stumbling and interruptions that have occurred when a group of people talks without any visual cues, has facilitated a different capacity across the group(s) to *enact* in the immediacy of everyday life. We noticed that after about six months of meeting this way, our collective discussions slowed—we said less and listened more; we waited and thought while online; we opened up pauses in the chatter and let the noises of transmission contribute to the resonating sonic space. In other words, *we engaged in the generation of consistency through techniques of group relation*. This consistency began to aggregate as we paid attention to the rhythms of voice, network transmission, ambient sound and noise. We moved with this polyrhythmicity and another kind of rhythm emerged that could not be heard but could certainly be felt.[28]

What Munster describes as a "generation of consistency" through attunement to a "kind of rhythm that could not be heard but could . . . be felt" is precisely incommunicational: it at once articulates knowledge as something that is shared and as something that is fundamentally singular in its medium specificity. Fathead follows in this vein, working as a lure for collective and collaborative incommunicational activities. The interrogations of the mediality of knowledge understood relationally—knowledge understood in its incommunicative technicities, especially with respect to scale—that come with Fathead-styled seminars work like the prosthetic device by amplifying, attenuating, navigating, and negotiating the excesses of infoldings, but this time in their collective and relational appearance. In short, the emphasis of Fathead has shifted from prosthetic doubling of individuals' perceptions toward pragmatic relational entanglements of collective human and nonhuman experiences. The simulational incongruencies— worked through relationally—thus appear not at all as technical failures but rather as the technical means through which the world's incongruency with itself collectivizes; that is, comes to experience—or rather, crafts a stratum of experience—rather than simply perception. These incongruencies are worldly incommunications, and the various Fathead undertakings each texture these differently.

To be clear, in conclusion: there is a pragmatic politics put to work in these experiences that is emphatically not simply seeking new ways to listen. It is true, certainly, that the pragmatics I've described (echoing

60   Chapter Two

Munster) is necessarily as critical as it is speculative, and that listening differently together uncovers entanglements and incongruencies that neoliberalism wants to elide, but on which it (like all experience) depends. More generally though, I am discussing the ways that communication, as a concept, is lived, with all the aschematic irreducibility that such living entails. Hence, my discussion of Fathead (and the project itself) isn't intended to show the cracks in our communicative apparatuses, but rather to attend to the possibilities that come with activating the metaphor (or really, with attuning to the metaphor's activity) of communication itself in its full impossibility.

3

Incomputable and Integral Incommunications

Chapter 2 details experiments with the technicity of listening that reach maturity less as prosthetic extensions and more as experiential knots that are textured by the specific technical relations of listening. This chapter advances that argument with a particular emphasis first on computation's incommunications, and proceeds to parse this particularity in the context of digital audio.

The fact that knowledge is always technically specified underwrites much of media theory. In recent years, significant attention has been given to the affordances that are opened in computational culture, especially by digital media. This attention has flourished, in part, because digital media involve microtemporal "technical operations [that] introduce levels of operationality that impact [human] experience without yielding any perceptual correlate."[1] That is, in contemporary technoculture the parts of our actions that exceed our conscious decision making are heightened by the premediating effects of algorithmic logics that are fundamentally alien to human cognition, even while algorithms directly impact how we think and act in our daily lives.

Computers make startlingly clear what was always the case, namely, that the world is not what it appears to be and indeed cannot be. Such worldly incoherence is incommunicated in human-computer coupling in obvious ways: for example, the operational speed of 3.8 billion cycles per second of the computer on which I'm writing greatly exceeds the possible speed of my conscious calculations. Likewise, the planetary (and beyond) infrastructure that networks computers—with networking by now a constitutive function of any computer—incants a form of information exchange that is definitively scaled beyond the perceptive apparatuses of human individuals: the scalar difference is a qualitative one because the globality of computational information exchange cannot be sensibly thought as an aggregate of local actions. Recalling the claim that "communication is the interactive computation of a reality," it is clear that there is a version of the globe that is called forth in and as global computation.[2] And finally, the legacy systems of computers work in a manner that echoes the precedential component of legal systems such that even at the level of code the functional scale of computer programs exceeds the capacities of human individuals.[3]

To be clear, these excesses are precisely the point of computers: they do what humans can't by working at scales that humans can't, and that is a large part of how they carve out their particular type of functionality. Computers are manifestly useful, and their navigation of these speeds and scales is a big reason why. Computational culture means that the microtemporal has become independently addressable and manipulable such that we can (as Mark Hansen suggests) dissociate sensibility from "the 'how' of experiencing."[4] Put simply, we can act on and in the world in ways that are scaled below (or beyond) our perceptual capacities. And yet, this suggests that to listen to computers in their incommunicative profiles is to go in search of the ways that the inverse is also the case: how might the bringing to sensibility of computation's contingency afford tentative purchase on a further expansiveness of the notion of "experience" that feeds back according to its own extended—rather than simply microtemporal—durations?

In my discussion of Fathead in chapter 2, I narrated the project's shift from experimenting with prosthetics to experimenting with situated relational sutures.[5] In order to stay with that narrative, I postponed mention of what was probably the most prominent constraint that I engaged in building the prototypes, namely, that they are made specifically for listening to single-source sounds, as opposed to listening environmentally or immersively. One can listen to an individual speaking or to a musical performance while wearing most versions of Fathead, but there are no versions of it that work (in any kind of comprehensible, consistent, and immersive way) as something that one could just wear all the time.

This is the case largely for technical reasons, and the particulars of the prototypes bear some attention in this respect. Consider two different ways that auditory scaling was approached. In the first, the sound levels of each microphone (which, remember, are worn on the ears) are compared to one another, with the relatively small difference in intensity then computed to add proportionate amplification and delays. That is, the difference in input volume between the two channels is taken to be indicative of the location of the sound source relative to the two ears. The single sound source is treated as a stereo (i.e., two-channel) input, with the difference between the two channels attributed to their travel from a single point of origin. This, of course, does not work if there are two physically separated sound sources, since the volume in each microphone will be the aggregate of the sources, thus affecting the placement of the individual sources in the thousand-foot virtual simulation.[6] By computing a single source as two channels of information, this approach allows for a mobile and wearable site of audition and a single moving sound source but is not in any meaningful sense a successful simulation that can be worn "in the wild."[7]

Conversely, another approach to making the Fathead prototypes was to use the single (mono) input of an iPod's built-in microphone, splitting the signal into two ("fake") stereo channels. In this case, the iPod is mounted to the top of the auditor's head, and the yaw sensor that is built into the iPod is accessed in order to track head movements on this axis, with the appropriate spatializing calculations thereby applied to the signal prior to its being sent to earphones: head rotations on the yaw axis move away from a center position that can be reset by tapping the iPod screen, which is programmed to behave as a recentering button. As a result, this approach treats the auditor as a series of fixed points of reception: the auditor can move and reset the center position, but the center position is always fixed rather than dynamic. Here again, the simulation only works for listening to a single audio source: the immersive auditory world is reduced to a mono source signal that is then doubled in order to be treated as a stereo signal,

64   Chapter Three

substituting a clear and fixed subject/object relation for the lived reality of enmeshed, dynamic, and coconstituting relations.

This decision to develop Fathead as a single-source listening device was largely dictated by technical constraints, and specifically by technicalities that exist precisely in and as something that we might think of as the causal infrastructure of computers. I demonstrated in chapter 2 the important understandings of sound that are opened by acknowledging that it is virtually impossible to create a responsive, mobile, wearable audio interface according to any scale but that of an actual listener's body. The technical constraints in developing Fathead extend these insights to computers, specifically by attesting to a general computational framework in which computers work as fundamentally grammatical machines that are hardwired for single inputs. Of course, one can have multiple, simultaneous computer interfaces, and even multiple input data sources. However, inputs become data in and as they are ordered by the computer, a transductive process that (ironically) enables them to be reordered (and otherwise recontextualized) in the computational ecology. Computers work via their own specific construction of linearity, and it is precisely this linearity that conditions the appearance of the opposite, namely, the hallucination of universal exchangeability that persists in data's afterlife.

To further understand this, it is worth remembering that it is only very late in the game that something like simultaneous multiperson editing of even a simple written computer document becomes an unremarkable undertaking. Online collaboration in Google Docs (then called Google Documents) wasn't publicly available until 2010. As recently as the early 2000s, I personally curtailed plans for a performance project that involved such technology because the cost of doing so would have been prohibitive and would even have required on-site technicians dedicated to maintaining the network. Even now, there is not to my knowledge a computer that will accept two mouse inputs at the same time; this is possible to do through software—and multiplayer online games accomplish this through networking—but it becomes massively inefficient.

One might be told that this inefficiency is the result of the hardware of individual computers simply not being designed for the task, but a more accurate explanation is that the hardware is exactly designed for the institution and preservation of message orders that come with managing inputs. Since inputs have to be managed relatively to one another, even a small number of additional inputs massively increases the amount of work a computer has to do in order to maintain the linear ordering on which computation depends: 2 inputs yield 2 possible orderings (i.e., permutations), 4 yield 24, 8 yield 40,320, and so forth. The inefficiency that comes with multiple inputs, then, is the result of the massive increase in ordering that is necessitated by the destabilization of a system/environment distinction that comes with any input, and upon which the linear ordering of computation depends. Put simply, a computer computes, first, by naturalizing a hard distinction between the computer and that which it computes, while simultaneously softening this distinction as a condition of its contact with the world. From this distinction, a coherent system of linear calculation becomes both possible and necessary; or rather (as will become clear), (im)possible and (un)necessary.

This reveals something of the specificity of computational linearity, which might be better thought as the computer's "time-criticality." Time-criticality is Wolfgang Ernst's nomination for the specific, operative dimensions that can be observed through analysis of the "tempor(e)alities" of technical signals rather than cultural signs.[8] For Ernst, the "oscillatory clock pulses [of digital computers] transformed time itself into information" such that "the material temporality of representational states [is liquidated] in favor of a purely logical *though electronically implemented* code."[9] The actual implementation of this "pure logic" is important, because it includes the latency of electronic and magnetic signals: functioning analogously to the speed of light, this latency constitutes the limit of computational (inter)action and thus grounds the causality through which computers proceed.

For example, Florian Sprenger extensively analyzes the role of time-criticality in computer network packet switching to show how a computer network's real-time activity in fact consists in such latencies, which he frames as "interruptions." Packet switching refers to the way that messages are sent on a distributed network, which essentially involves breaking individual messages into component parts (i.e., packets) that are sent on separate paths through a mesh of nodes. Each time a packet arrives at a node, a message containing timing information is sent back to the node from which it came so that the network can synchronize and optimize the routes that packets follow (while still keeping them distinct, and thus unsusceptible to any single disruptive event). As Sprenger explains (citing also

Peter Galison), "by equipping packets with information about their transmission times and using this information to update [the] network [the network design is faced with the] fundamental physical problems of relativity and synchronization: the transmission of this information, which is supposed to be used simultaneously to ascertain the present state of the nodes, itself requires time."[10] As a result, "realtime can only mean that signals are arriving at the speed in which they can be processed as quickly as possible. . . . Two processes or events are therefore synchronous if they do not exceed the interval of time that is required for a technical process to run [such that] every act of synchronization contains a remnant of timebound transmission."[11] Sprenger parses this as a reduction of "time-critically differing temporalities to a single denominator" in order to emphasize that true simultaneity is never achieved.[12] There is always an interruption in the network's networking.

However, the opposite is also the case. Sprenger observes that "synchronization is the coordination of multiple levels of time [that operationally harmonizes] various technical orders in an effort to operate with differences."[13] From this, we can note that the reduction of temporalities that Sprenger observes is itself productive of the computer network's tempor(e)ality. Indeed, this is precisely what synchronization or simultaneity means in any informatic context: *simultaneous* isn't some abstract state, but instead is a pragmatic concept that names the temporal threshold beneath which a difference does not make a difference to a system.[14] To note as much is not to deny the existence of microdifferences, but rather to open the possibility of conceptualizing the computer network in its own specific tempor(e)ality. It is only by acknowledging operational synchronization that computer networks (and indeed, computers more generally) can be engaged in terms that draw out their differences, not least because what counts as linear follows from what counts as synchronized, and what counts as causally determinant follows from both of these. Time-critical operations are productive of tempor(e)alities for precisely this reason: they describe and perform precise and specific versions of causality.

If computers—which are both the spine and the skin of global communications networks—are in some important sense linear machines, it is worth noting that this is both the problem and the achievement of computation: the genius of computation lies in the specific time-criticality through

Incomputable and Integral Incommunications   67

which this linearity is enacted both because it is no small technical feat and, more important, because it is a linearity that is grounded in contingency and productive of dynamism. In this respect, computers are similar to language. Language doesn't work by reducing some prior, pure, natural experience that precedes it, but is rather complexly and multicausally entangled in experiential ecologies of which it is both cause and effect (and other things as well); just as that is the case with language, so too is it the case with computation.

M. Beatrice Fazi makes this point forcefully, and in doing so contributes enormously to contemporary debates that aim to unfold the most fruitful ways to think through the specific affordances and constraints of computation. Fazi's work in this area is particularly notable for its sensitivity to the vagaries of aesthetic discourse (in the best senses), working always in the direction of mining computers for that in them which resists understanding in other settings.[15] That is, Fazi listens attentively to the incommunications of computers by registering specifically what she calls their "internal contingency" as a constitutive feature of computation more broadly, and one that is central to any aesthetic inquiry of and into computation.

To this end, in an article titled "Incomputable Aesthetics: Open Axioms of Contingency," Fazi insists that there is an indeterminacy "proper to the formal, logical, quantitative character of computation."[16] Fazi begins her argument with Kurt Gödel's (1931) famous "this statement is false" proof, which demonstrates that all formal axiomatic systems are incomplete. Specifically, Gödel shows that in any axiomatic system there will be "propositions that cannot be proved or disproved within the system in question," or, as Luciana Parisi states, "any set of instructions is conditioned by what can't be calculated."[17] Importantly, such propositions emerge within the axiomatic system itself: in being precisely statements of the type that the system's axioms are designed to differentiate, they are fully dataphasic incommunications. That is, Gödel's theorem is aimed not at proving the existence of externalities to a given system (as in, for example, a sentence such as, "The weather is 173") and likewise not at proving the existence of internal incompatibilities (e.g., "The weather is false"), but rather at demonstrating something of a blind spot that is enacted in and as the axioms themselves: "This sentence is false" only reaches its vexatious, paradoxical, and dataphasic fate within the (recursively) axiomatic system that it enacts. It is a kind of logical stutter.

With this in mind, Fazi notes the historical and conceptual connection between Gödel's theorem and Alan Turing's 1936 investigation into the "possibility of finding a mechanical, finite-step and formally expressed process that would set the standard for deductive procedures"; the latter would arguably ultimately produce modern computers, insofar as computers are defined through their completion of tasks that are "recursively axiomatizable."[18] Together, then, Gödel and Turing help conceptualize computers as (imaginary) machines wherein a function being defined is applied within its own definition.

I would note that, in this sense, computers are fundamentally pragmatic: in alignment with the pragmatic maxim rejecting the idea that there are facts which are unknowable in principle, computers proceed by doing what they can do and define themselves through this procedure.[19] This means computers have a complicated relation to representation: N. Katherine Hayles, for example, developed the concept of "flickering signifiers" to account for the "productive force" of computer code as a pattern (as opposed to a presence), and specifically as an analytic for understanding the immanence between what code says and does.[20] As Hayles (and many others after her) emphasize, the entanglement of code and its enaction makes the former a particularly queer sort of (representational) language.

Historically, similar questions were being asked in the realm of mathematics as computers were initially being conceived. In particular, the intuitionist mathematics (a branch of mathematical constructivism) of L. E. J. Brouwer instigates many of the key insights that came to define computation's pragmatic disposition, and Brouwer's intuitionism was evidently on Gödel's mind as he developed the work that would be so influential to Turing. To understand intuitionism, one must first grasp constructivism's more general departure from classical mathematics. As Robert Goldblatt notes, in classical mathematics "an 'existence proof' often proceeds by showing that the assumption of the non-existence of an entity of a certain kind leads to contradiction."[21] That is, if something not existing is logically untenable, then it follows (in classical logic) that that thing must exist. This view—called the law of the excluded middle—is disputed by constructivists, who argue that "a statement is the record of a construction" rather than a revelation of an acontextual and unmediated truth, so that "asserting the truth of *a* amounts to saying 'I have made a (mental) construction of that which *a* describes.'"[22] As a result, logical contradiction "is not a proof of existence at all, since the latter, to be legitimate, must explicitly exhibit the particular object in question."[23] In short—echoing a logic of negative dialectics—to "say that a is not true means only that I have not at this time constructed a, which is not the same as saying a is false."[24] In this way, Brouwer not only rejected nonconstructive mathematical arguments, but moreover denied "traditional logic as a valid representation of mathematical reasoning."[25] With respect to the latter, Brouwer observed that logical "laws" were developed by abstracting from mathematical deductions that were themselves developed at a time when mathematics was only concerned with the world of the finite, and are thus not suitable within the expanded purview of contemporary mathematics. Paraphrasing Gregory Bateson, we might say that Brouwer diagnosed an application of mathematics that was developed before the mathematics was ripe to be applied.[26]

Whereas "classical mathematics uses logic to generate theorems," intuitionism holds "that there are no non-experienced truths and that logic is not an absolutely reliable instrument to discover truths."[27] Brouwer thus maintained that the source of mathematical truth is found in our primary intuitions about mathematical objects: through theorems deduced "by means of introspective construction."[28] This is not, importantly, akin to claiming that mathematics is dependent on language: for Brouwer, language has a "practical function in describing and communicating, but is not prerequisite to the activity of performing mental constructions" because the essential content of mathematics remains intuitive rather than formal.[29] In this sense, mathematics is an "activity—autonomous, self-sufficient, and not dependent on language."[30]

Taken together, this reveals what are called the "two acts" of intuitionism, which together clarify the conceptual invariances between intuitionism, computation (and computability), and pragmatism. The "first act" is an intuitive "construction in the mind of 'two-ness,'" which amounts to the ability to temporally distinguish one thing from another: for Brouwer, our direct awareness of "two states of mind, one succeeding the other, lies at the heart of our intuition of objects."[31] In tandem with this temporal (if extralinguistic, in Brouwer's—arguably reductive—sense of language) construction of objects, the "second act" recognizes the possibility of repeating these constructions. As a result, Goldblatt explains, "There is no such thing to the intuitionist as an actual completed infinite collection. However, by the generation of endlessly proceeding sequences we are led

70   Chapter Three

to a mathematics of the potentially infinite, as embodied in the notion of constructions which, although finite at any given stage, can be continued in an unlimited fashion."[32] In this, the connection that intuitionism forges between computation and pragmatism is brought into sharp relief: we can understand computers as (among other things) a pragmatic enaction of intuitionist logic.[33]

It is in this pragmatic context that, as Fazi notes, Turing demonstrated that some functions cannot be computed, and indeed that the "formal notion of computation" requires such incomputable functions. Dataphasia conditions the computer's enunciative capacities. That is, Turing proved that "there is no algorithm (i.e. no effective method) that can decide, in advance of its calculation, whether a statement is true or false, and he did so by demonstrating that there are some tasks that cannot be accomplished by his universal computing machines. These problems are said to be *incomputable functions* with no solution."[34]

Functions and their (in)computability bear on the question of infinity, so understanding the distinction between infinitude and innumerability is central to this discussion. In essence, an innumerable value is a value that can be calculated indefinitely, like pi. That is, one can calculate pi by dividing the circumference of a circle by its diameter—that is, pi is a calculable value—but there is no limit to the specificity of this calculation, which can therefore go on indefinitely. An infinitude, by contrast, is an abstraction, and in that sense cannot be calculated. Innumerable values can be calculated with endless specificity but are not themselves infinite since they only go on insofar as they are actually calculated. With this in mind, we can say that to compute is to parse an abstract infinitude in terms of a concrete innumerability.

Computation thus actualizes uniquely and specifically. In this respect, we are compelled to recognize the importance of computation's aesthetic grounding: computation isn't analogous to other rational processes and cannot be represented, but rather "computation is computation."[35] For Fazi, this means there is an ontological contingency to computation that precedes its contact with the world. In saying this, she of course notes the oft-remarked-upon fact that any computation is incomplete because no rational calculation can ever explain and encompass every element of actuality. That is, it is clear that any opening of computation to its phenomenal, worldly outside will necessarily involve selective processes in terms of both the breadth and the depth of contact—where a frame is drawn and how detailed the resolution inside the frame will be. Indeed, this form of contingency comes with any determination of the world, and computation is no exception: the world can never be fully determined because (among other reasons) to do so would require the determination itself to be part of the determining.

However, while the contingency that comes from the externality of any systemic closure is well-trod territory, Fazi adds the insistence that there is a prior and more foundational contingency that is specifically internal to computation in the form of the incomputability upon which Turing insisted. This internal contingency flows from the fact that "computation *is made up of* . . . quantities that cannot be fully counted":[36] to Fazi's ontological claim that "computation is computation" we can thus now add the post-Luhmannian observation that even though computation is incomputable, computers nonetheless compute. To attempt to account for computation is to attempt to account for the specific decisions that constitute a computational system, which themselves are enacted in a time-critical context of undecidability. Thus, for Fazi, "rules have a level of contingency that does not depend on the empirical outside of the formal axiomatic system."[37] From this—in a twist on Wittgenstein's insistence that every well-founded belief rests on a belief that is not founded—she demonstrates that there is nothing very irrational in incomputability. Rather, for Fazi the "incomputable is an excess of reason, not the lack thereof" because incomputability is the ongoing generation of the inexhaustibility of the operations of discretization that are, in fact, computation.[38] Incomputability points to computers being actual processors of innumerable values, rather than ideal conceptualizations of infinite ones. Put differently, computation is constitutively processual and rational, and the combination of these modes produces a form of rationality that is excessive (i.e., incomputable) when viewed nonprocessually (i.e., from outside the formal system). Incomputability is a kind of internal incommunication specific to the rationality of computation and is therefore, in this sense, dataphasic.

Describing this incomputability is a complex task. However, the incomputability itself is simply a fact, and one that has recognizable pragmatic effects: Fazi notes, for example, that "it is because of incomputability that, to this day, there does not exist a one hundred per cent 'bug-free' program. The correctness of a piece of software cannot be finally determined"

72   Chapter Three

because it can only be checked through a computer program that executes the code to be tested in a line-by-line, processual manner. As a result, "the [innumerable] possibilities of endless axiomatic loops in a program are beyond the finiteness of the time-constrained procedure constructed to infer its fallacy."[39]

There is an important understanding of scale and experience that underwrites Fazi's argument, and specifically one that aligns with Ernst's media-archaeological understanding of time-critical media, parsed quite eloquently by Hansen in his contribution to the 2017 *Philosophy after Nature* collection. In the Ernst-Hansen view, time-criticality acts "as the performative hinge linking micro- and macro worlds."[40] That is, time-criticality names the fact that "mathematics must always be implemented in a physical materiality [consuming at least] a minimal time interval" in order to convert signals into phenomenologically accessible forms.[41] In this way, time-critical media have an "onto-performative" power that is akin to that described by Fazi with respect to computation, in that time-critical media do not "sample from a pre-existent and standing time but from the physical processes that are, as it were, *underneath* time";[42] this "underneath" of time echoes what Fazi describes as computation's "internality." The actual operation is one wherein an abstraction is brought into being in such a way that it henceforth cannot exist or have existed outside of the finitude of its operation. Just as computation is the enaction of incomputability for Fazi, *time* for Hansen and Ernst is the specific, processual technical actualization that it names.

Hansen's reading of Ernst is subsequently extended to a critique of Timothy Morton's concept of the hyperobject. Without unnecessarily detailing that critique, it bears noting that, contra Morton, Hansen adopts a majority view of Niels Bohr's account of quantum indeterminacy: Hansen insists that quantum mechanics—that is, the resolution of quantum indeterminacy— is time-critical because it is "identical to the actual implementation of the quantum leap in a material substrate."[43] For Hansen, "there can be no reference beyond what is given in the measuring experiment" so that we are "left with a *probabilistic* analysis of the possible outcomes of quantum experimentation, [where] . . . probability does not index a closed set of variables that [could be fully known] but rather an open, and radically indeterminate set of possible outcomes."[44] Ultimately, Hansen concludes that "the quantum phenomena produced through the technology of measurement *are ontological:* they are manifestations of the structure of the world as it is, and they are the only way in which the world *is.*"[45]

In sum, Ernst, Hansen, and Fazi would agree that there is a qualitative difference between the microtime of time-critical processes such as computation, and what Ernst calls the "macrotime of media history."[46] Moreover, this difference is a hierarchical one for them, similar to that between the intact world of classical physics and the microworld of quantum physics: it isn't that two different physics are at work, but rather that quantum indeterminacy is always already resolved at the point of its observation, its mechanics. Likewise, the macrotime of history is, in this view, an expression of the microtemporal operations that ontologically precede it even if those operations are only sensible as such through their having agglomerated. And finally, the three thinkers converge on the position that this difference between the micro and macro is onto-performative and therefore cannot be abstracted.

It is this way of distinguishing between the micro and macro that illuminates something of computation's dataphasic incommunications, especially the paradox of scale that the distinction articulates. To put it simply, thinking computation incommunicatively necessitates refusing an understanding of scale that would make it simply a measure: there is no fully objective perspective from which a micro/macro distinction can be sustained, much less one through which the micro should be prioritized. Instead, we should understand scale as a pragmatic concept that affords a transversal thinking of the coimbrication of micro and macro operations: these operations are material-semiotically recursive, crafting the scale that would be their measure. And indeed, this plays out in the actual operations of computers in the way that resources are allocated: microcomputational processes in a computer always involve a macrocomputational assessment and prioritization of available resources (i.e., computing power, memory, and temperature, as well as battery power and archiving in personal computers).[47] In this way, micro and macro are qualitatively distinct concepts that are brought into relation through the scaling operations of computation, rather than preexisting them. For this reason (among others), I emphatically disagree with what I read as a prioritization of the micro that is seeded throughout Hansen's work, as evidenced for example in the claim that macroscale operations "belong to a later stage of analysis [than microscale ones because they] address a higher order of being than the production of sensibility."[48]

This pragmatic indeterminacy is crucial to understanding the constellation of thinkers in the argument at hand, in whose work the distinction between micro and macro is at once denied (because there is only one physics) and insisted upon (because the cut between micro and macro is precisely the work of time-critical media). Indeed, articulating the paradox of this position is precisely the accomplishment of both the constellation itself and each thinker within it. Hansen (writing through Ernst) and Fazi each work through this problem by insisting on a certain kind of performativity: the authors don't insist that there are transcendental, categorical micro and macro scales, but rather that technical activities bring about causal relations that are both particular to the internal dynamic of their enaction and prior to, and establishing of, their enactive possibilities.

For Hansen and for Fazi—two very different thinkers, in many respects—this weird temporality is part and parcel of a Whiteheadian worldly sensibility to which we are granted technical access, and indicative (especially for Hansen) of a priority of the microscale. But this might be thought differently as the dataphasic incommunications of a technical world that is always in excess and out of joint with itself. The speculative twist of this approach would emphasize that there must necessarily exist a temporality that calls forth the experimental setup as such, as one possibility among others, such that this setup must be situated both prior to and after the dynamic interacting technical temporalities that craft a cut between scales. This understanding further expands the weird temporality of incommunication that invests technicity, because it means that micro and macro scales don't just coproduce one another, they are also in dynamic relation with the medium-specific measure (i.e., scale) that at once differentiates and conjoins them. Such a temporality would be an aesthetic one, operating according to and in excess of the logics that at once describe computers, underwrite them, and undermine any invocations of computational meaning.

Because computers are pragmatic machines—formed in the forge of intuitionism—we can leverage tangible insights into the materials and materialities that they process by latching on to the particularities of their conjunctions. With that in mind, the remainder of this chapter focuses on what we can hear of computational incommunication specifically as it operates in digital audio. How do the machinations of computers impact their processing of sound, and what can we learn from this?

The actual indeterminacy that Fazi locates at the heart of computation has its correlate in digital audio in the form of the Fourier transform. Developed at the beginning of the nineteenth century, the transform precedes both computers and their conceptualization. However, the advent of computation massively amplifies the sampling logic of the Fourier transform: the incredibly fast and highly developed processes of discretization through which computers compute makes them the ultimate sampling machines. Indeed, the most common way to think about the difference between digital and analog technologies works along precisely these lines: analog technologies work by transducing energy from medium to medium, whereas digital technologies work by grammatizing events as context-independent information through a series of informatic snapshots. As Alex Galloway contends, the Fourier transform is thus the place from which digitality comes, because it effectively discretizes an analog signal.[49]

The Fourier transform is at the core of Fourier analysis/resynthesis, and the latter means in the realm of audio that any sound can theoretically be synthesized with a degree of fidelity equal to the fidelity of the "source" audio. This analysis/resynthesis is accomplished by transforming the time-domain waveform of the original sound into a series of frequency-domain values that are played back using oscillators, like a flipbook animation. This means that the timbre of a simple sound such as a sustained pitch on a violin can be analyzed in terms of the relative strength of the various overtones (otherwise known as partials) that make up the harmonic series.[50] Through this technique, the composite sound of a violin can thus be resynthesized as a series of simultaneous component sounds, namely the overtones of which it consists: "what was once wholly analog may now be defined in terms of a sum of digital elements; what was once a continuous wave is now a series of discrete coefficients."[51] In many senses, the Fourier transform acts analogously to the way that a prism diffracts a beam of light into its component parts, and indeed timbre is often treated as though it is synonymous with color. Analyzing and resynthesizing a sound, then, is similar to representing the purple of a given iris in terms of its intensities of red and blue, and subsequently re-creating this color by mixing these primary colors accordingly. Just as an iris's color isn't a solid block, even sustained sounds are rarely simple and static and, moreover, most sounds undergo significant timbral changes over the course of their articulation: for example, the moment that a violin's bow touches the string sounds timbrally distinct from the moment that immediately follows.[52]

All of this relates to why I explained the project life cycle of Fathead in chapter 2: the logic of fidelity that I've rehearsed above is precisely what seduced me into my initial impulse to think of the project as an interesting individual prosthetic, rather than in the ecological terms at which I ultimately arrived. Put simply, the concept of fidelity mobilized in the above narrative of digital audio aligns with the computational mode of appearance that suggests universal scalability and exchangeability, ultimately arriving at a fiction of pure data. That story isn't wrong per se, but it is neither the whole story nor the only story that can be told.

Recall that for something to be properly computational, it has to engage the contingent actuality of (in)computability. This paradox emerges in digital audio as follows: on one hand, it is manifestly true that any sound can theoretically be analyzed and resynthesized at full fidelity, because the process of digitization parses sound as information and thus crafts it as a problem of information capture. In this framing, one might never digitize a sound at full fidelity, but this does not undermine the logic through which one could; any shortcomings, in other words, would be quantitative. On the other hand, this is not—and can never be!—actually the case, and in a very real sense the impossibility of this actualization comes about not only because of the contingencies of the world, but more fundamentally via a theoretical aporia at the heart of the actual process of digitization itself: namely, analyzing and resynthesizing at full fidelity comes up against the obvious technical limitation of requiring a potentially infinite number of oscillators, each of which is capable of being controlled at an infinitely fine grain and synchronized with infinite (as opposed to time-critical) exactitude. The infinitude of this problem is crucial, because it treats the computer as an abstraction, ignoring its specific time-critical operations—and these operations are exactly what makes a computer a computer! As explained above, infinity is not computable as such, and thus must be parsed by a computer as a concrete innumerability. Hence the genius of the Fourier transform—which features innumerabilities, specifically in its use of the

Fourier integral—is to afford a computational solution by substituting the actual innumerability and nonperiodic possibilities of real numbers for the formal infinitude that fidelity to wave spectra would require.

Full fidelity is thus analogous to synchronization as discussed above (via Sprenger), naming the actual, time-critical operations of the computer rather than a transcendental state. To make the point more forcefully: we can only properly say that any sound can be "theoretically" analyzed and resynthesized at full fidelity by adding scare quotes: a pragmatic disposition makes it clear that the actual limitations are themselves there in theory too, because they are part of the formal axiomatic system. As Fazi makes clear for us, the actual impossibility of full fidelity comes about not just from contact with the outside world but also from the contingencies internal to the computation of digital audio.

This brings the paradox of digital audio to a point: through the concept of full fidelity, the Fourier transform enables the periodization of the nonperiodizable. It does this by substituting the material innumerability of real numbers for the formal infinitude of a series. The Fourier transform thus produces an analysis/resynthesis that is temporalized in the materiality of real numbers, and thus adheres to what Hansen calls the "law of temporal finitude"—namely, that "time is always temporalized in material processes."[53] However, it does so in a way that does not diminish in fidelity at finer scales because it uses real numbers that are nonperiodic. Thus, as Hansen puts it, "the hard time introduced by Fourier integrals inscribes time as periodicity and thereby introduces irreversibility through a 'physical' or 'material' symbolization that has no need for any human contribution."[54] This is both the time-criticality of digital audio and how it incommunicates.

It bears noting that the broader concept of fidelity has been widely critiqued in sound studies (and elsewhere), and has been convincingly recast by a number of thinkers as a concept that articulates a deeply fraught set of sociopolitical ideals as much as any particular technical accomplishment. That is, to speak of fidelity in any sense is to invoke the position and constitution of an ideal listener, and all of the racist, sexist, ableist, and classist biases that entails; such arguments are at this point uncontroversial and irrefutable.[55] What I aim to add to this is an incommunicative echo of Fazi's argument about computation that insists that even if the principles of an ideal listener and listening position were adopted, fidelity would remain

78   Chapter Three

a technically contingent operation in and as its actual (and therefore also theoretical) computation. As a result, critiques of the ideal listener can be based not only in the (crucially important) logics of critical identity politics and in sociomaterial practices of listening, but also in the materiality of computation. The constitutive (technical) incommunication of computation echoes in the sociopolitical register in which the ideal listener is situated, laying bare the latter's ideological constitution.

What follows from the above analysis is a renewed attention to the scalar incommunications that come about with digital audio: the specific performative excesses that come about in the disjunctive conjunctions of sound and computation. Several years ago, I approached this problem pragmatically by undertaking an experiment that routed a single twenty-minute audio recording to four different Fourier transforms, subsequently fed the resynthesized twenty minutes back again and again into the same transform, and then repeated the process for one week (i.e., for 168 hours, or approximately 504 repetitions). In Fourier transforms, the rate of sampling and the window size (i.e., the length of each sample) work in tandem to produce what is called the spectrum resolution of the analysis; in this case, each of the four Fourier transforms had different window sizes and sample rates, but in a way that amounted to them each having the same resulting spectrum resolution. That is, the four transforms were measurably the same quality, but according to qualitatively different measures: they were technically different, akin to the way that four students might each earn the same grade on a test while having answered the actual questions of the test differently.

In the case of my experiment, these technical differences became notably audible over the course of the week. The recordings each ended up sounding like feedback hums (rather than resembling the original source audio), as one would expect, but the hums settled at different pitches in each of the Fourier transforms.[56] This exemplifies in digital audio, then, the actuality of computation upon which Fazi insists, and which time-criticality describes in media more generally: what ultimately becomes audible are the particular operations of the computer vis-à-vis the audio.

Against this understanding, those policing the terrain of computer science might bring up the role of different approaches to windowing, which involves smoothing the cutoffs of samples by altering the amplitude at their edges and then overlapping consecutive samples.[57] The use of such windows would effectively prevent the signal degradation that leads to the hums, and at the time of the experiment I was told by one such expert that my exploration was disingenuous because I didn't make use of this technique. However, when considering the internality of computational contingency it is worth noting that windowing is as much an art as a science because it involves a subjective assessment of the type and scale of the desired outcome of the signal processing rather than, say, an analysis based on an objective notion of fidelity (which objectivity is impossible in any case).[58] More to the point, it is also the case that windowing doesn't technically correct errors but rather introduces redundancies that override the deviations that come about as a result of computational contingency. As such, windowing is literally a convolution of computation's processual excesses, and thus evinces something in the computational process that is entirely specific to it.

All that being the case, two points of emphasis that diverge from (though don't contradict) Fazi's computational description bear noting: first, it is not the case—or at least, not only the case—that the differences that lead to the hums accrue little by little in each repetition, such that one might say that they are there from the beginning in their final form and simply become larger with each repetition. Instead, a weirder—internally incommunicative—process is in play, because much of what is different are artifacts of the feedback process itself. Since the hums come from the act of computing, they are a product of the weird tempor(e)ality of computation: the macro of the repetition is in an important sense after and before the ongoing production of the computational micro. (As discussed above, for example, the computing of previous computations affects the computer's allocation of labor and resources in ways that produce the audible differences that will have been there from the beginning.) This draws on a lesson from various forms of glitch art: the experimental boundaries needed to secure a finite and strictly causal relation are always procedurally constituted, because to compute is literally to work procedurally. As a result, the interior space of a computer is always both in flux and operative in relation to these fluctuations such that temporalities (and causalities) of glitches are internally multidirectional.[59]

Really, even if computers were deterministic systems, that wouldn't mean they would be predictable. This points to the second line of divergence from Fazi, which flows from the first: it is also not possible to secure a pure interiority of computation. This has been argued via the interactionist paradigm in the philosophy of computation, which holds that it is not always appreciated that the Church-Turing thesis on computability "applies only to computation of functions, rather than to all computation. Function-based computation transforms a finite input into a finite output in a finite amount of time, in a closed-box fashion. By contrast, the general notion of computation includes arbitrary procedures and processes—which may be open, non-terminating, and involving multiple inputs interleaved with outputs."[60] More generally, though, we can observe that insofar as computation is definitionally pragmatic—insofar, that is, as computation is defined through its actualization of the question of (in)computability—we can simply insist that to compute is always in some sense to compute an exteriority; or, really, to compute that of an exteriority that is always already internal in and as the trans-sub/ob-jective dimension of its experience. In the example in question, the exteriority is a sound, and noting the porousness of the computational interior again aligns with a perspective that has been widely developed with respect to the concept of fidelity.[61] Once more, the technicalities of computation are inseparable from sociopolitical concerns.

Moreover, in considering specifically digital audio, this spatial contamination evinces a temporal one: we might say that it is because it is impossible to secure a pure interior that microcomputation will always bear a trace of both the macrotemporality of computation and the macrotemporality that is its outside. Remembering again the role of resource allocation and prioritization to computation, we can recognize incommunicative excesses—be they glitches or hums—as part and parcel of a material logic of the computer that is at once internal and external: internal because it *is* the computation (as Fazi identifies) and external because its computing doesn't just accept inputs but actually experiences itself in and as the processuality of actual and finite material circumstances (including, importantly, electricity).

If the above observations can often be applied to computation more generally, the case of digital audio is nonetheless particularly instructive because the oft-remarked features of sound—its being immersive, relational, and so forth—tend to fall apart in the context of its computation.[62] This is because audio computation imagines communication in terms of mecha-

Incomputable and Integral Incommunications   81

nistic (audible) signals, but we know (from Michel Serres and others) that audibility as it pertains to an ear is instead a vanishing point of communication into a series of black boxes (i.e., rather than being a threshold) that both depend on and undermine the distinction between sender and receiver: to account for the private dimension of a listening ear is to acknowledge that the occult workings of this interiority are inseparable from the objective messages that are exterior to it.[63]

Indeed, in binaural listening the intensive vanishing act performed in and as the moment and point of reception skitters over to the other ear to deafen it extensively: it does so physically by shadowing certain frequencies (which is partially how sound is spatialized in binaural animals, including humans), but more importantly literally because when the same sound is heard binaurally such that a certain degree of difference obtains with respect to volume, the quieter channel sometimes becomes inaudible. Likewise, Mack Hagood notes (for example) a case where an audiometric testing signal sent to a subject's right ear is matched in pitch and intensity to their experience of tinnitus (i.e., a persistent ringing in their ear) in their left ear, and results in their no longer being able to differentiate between the two sounds.[64] As these examples illustrate, one ear's endless string of black boxes precludes, under certain conditions, the emergence of the initial conditions for even the question of communication in the other ear. Stereo listening is a collective incommunicative system predicated not just on a difference between its component parts (i.e., between each of a listener's ears), but also on an inhibiting mechanism between them: I know that my ears are working when, under certain conditions, I do not hear in one ear what I know I should have.

The point is: a sound's audibility is relative not just to the sensitivity of the receiving apparatus but also to something in that apparatus's incommunicative framework. It follows that audibility cannot be understood exclusively in terms of isolatable properties; it cannot be fully datafied any more than data can be fully audified. More than this, this irreducible relationality is constitutively obscured in that it operates precisely in and as a black box of intracochlear communication. And so, this is part of why (as I mentioned with Fathead) it is virtually impossible to create a responsive, mobile, wearable audio interface according to any scale but that of the actual listener's body. It is not just for phenomenological reasons that one can't computationally simulate hearing like an owl, but also that it quite literally

82   Chapter Three

doesn't compute. To compute this incommunicative system would depend on a relational understanding of information that is anathema to the computer's logic of universal exchange.

Put differently, the particular aural incommunications that are referenced in concepts such as resonance are not and cannot be captured in computational logics of scale: it doesn't make sense to speak of resonance in terms of either the nestings or parallelisms that contour the computational topography, and that must be taken for granted in order for computers to (in)communicate. Thus, I concur with Fazi that "the limits of computation" are not really limits, but rather "the mark of computation's potentiality."[65] However, this potentiality proceeds internally to precisely the extent that it excludes specific externalities—which is not to say externality in general—in order to constitute itself; it is, in short, the ongoing, processual production of differential excesses that specifically texture the invariant appearances that they simultaneously enact. This, at least, is how a Fourier transform works, which is to say how it incommunicates.

In sum, data (grasped as an audio problem) and sound (grasped as a data problem) reveal incommunication as constitutive of listening and computation. In this, we can understand digital audio as a process that crafts a material analogy between the gap between human ears and the structural contingency of computation. A spatial gap between ears (and the tempor(e)ality it creates) facilitates a sense of immersion and simultaneity and therefore incommunicates the outside world in certain ways. Computers do something similar, actualizing innumerabilities in ways that can seem to produce abstract infinitudes. Computers also lay bare a difference at the heart of both operations that is idealized into fidelity (for sound) and universality (for data/information), and that difference materially and pragmatically grounds a critical politics that works against ideality, universality, and universal exchangeability by insisting on the aesthetic excesses that these ceaselessly produce.

4

Algorithms, Art, and Sonicity

The communication that is community exceeds the horizon of signification.

JEAN-LUC NANCY, QUOTED IN PATRICIA CLOUGH, *THE USER UNCONSCIOUS*

Chapter 3 examines the specific, subperceptual operations of computation (especially with respect to digital audio), cautions against giving ontological priority to microscales over macroscales, and points to the strange interscalar relations that become apparent when we no longer imagine the world as first composed of small units from which larger entities aggregate. This chapter forwards that argument by parsing these computational logics through artistic practices that demonstrate the sense in which temporality, in its incommunicativeness, is an aesthetic mode. That is, with its characteristic coupling of human activity with unthinkable machinic speeds and scales, contemporary technoculture intensifies the basic but essential incommunicative problem of how to act responsibly when one's actions are implicated in nonlinear networks that exceed the purview of consciousness. This chapter pragmatically listens alongside the ways that art has textured this bind by bringing aesthetic practices to bear on digital technologies and to the algorithms through which they operate.

Listening plays a key role in this context because it is not only possible to listen to visual processes but arguably necessary to develop nonvisual techniques for steering human-technology coupling. For better and worse, becoming agential through distributed attunement is a key strategy for addressing the unvisualizably immense and minute scales that subtend so many of our contemporary experiences. Today more than ever, visuality is less about literal seeing and more geared toward organizing the world according to a particular logic that exceeds a simply "analytic predisposition for culturally informed arrangements of light."[1] The phenomena that vision addresses need not be visible. For example, DNA is literally and constitutively invisible, since it is smaller than the wavelength of light and therefore will not reflect light no matter how much it is magnified.[2] Nonetheless, numerous technical accomplishments are premised on DNA looking the way that we've visualized it, which is testament to vision's migration beyond its own enabling conditions (namely, reflected light). Notably, this is also the case for nanotechnology, and applies similarly to phenomena ranging from computer processor speeds to global warming to distributed communications networks.

Sound opens a particularly promising field of possibilities in this context: if sound, after all, "undermines form, as stable referent, by always moving away from its source, while slipping past the guide of representational meaning by exceeding the symbolic," then to listen is to become sensitive to this recondite economy.[3] Listening is a dynamic process of learning and self-development where sense resounds beyond significance,[4] and aurality encompasses practices that make literal use of sound but also extends to listening itself as a comportment toward attunement. To invoke sound in this way is thus emphatically not to suggest that it presents some sort of metaphysical alternative to the (not actually existing) "visual dominance of Western culture," nor is it to take up a position as to whether this approach yields an analysis that successfully departs from the spurious power relations of normative neoliberal (techno)culture. Rather, it is simply to suggest that the material semiotics of aurality might differently activate aesthetic scenarios in such ways that they can be put on the move in different registers, toward different ends.

Algorithms, Art, and Sonicity   85

To begin, consider Kelly Egan's five-minute film *Ransom Notes*, which features a series of letters (and letter-like shapes) appearing and disappearing against a black background that is subtly textured with visual noise, accompanied by a soundtrack consisting of regularly metered staccato beeps, resembling an overdriven Morse code transmitter.[5] We could begin to think about this at a basic level of representation, of course, asking after the details of the film in terms of their meaning. That is, we might note the specific letters, the typeface, the letters' position on the screen, their correspondence with the sound, and so forth, and proceed to connect it to the world—or at least a world—outside of the film. Indeed, meaning is always about such couplings, and in this case we could (and should) historicize this initial representational reading by understanding that the piece was a response to the G20 protests that took place in Toronto, Canada, in 2010. Moreover, we could look to the didactics of the piece, online information about it and the protests, and so forth to understand what that connection means for Egan and her work.

Having opened such an analysis, we could then thicken the reading substantially through more specific attention to the materials that Egan uses in the film, and to what they tell us about how it was made. Such an approach would lead to a discussion of Egan's use of direct sound, for example, where she makes actual, physical inscriptions on the optical soundtrack of the film to create the work's sound. We would also note that *Ransom Notes* is made on 35 mm film, which not only has a very specific look and feel to it but also more readily affords certain sorts of content and constrains others, offers certain advantages in terms of preservation, and has specific technical limitations in terms of how (and consequently where) it is shown. In turn, we could (and should) historicize this material vector of analysis by situating the piece in the broader history of material practices of laboring with film: rather than just issuing from a single creator, such practices are often collaborative and reiterative, such that the history of 35 mm film is as much a history of invisible labor as it is one of creative expression per se. Moreover, we could note at the same time that this is a 35 mm film made in 2011, which situates these material considerations somewhat differently, and which also allows me to write about the film here despite its relative obscurity (i.e., because I know that curious readers can click the footnoted link and see it—or rather a video of it—themselves).

86   Chapter Four

All of the above is worthwhile analysis, would get us some way into thinking about the film, and would also demonstrate the necessity of the conjunctive term "material-semiotics," as it is immediately clear that our representational and material analyses can't really be separated out from one another. However, something basic would still be missing in our understanding, which is something about what we might think of as the logic of the piece: the successive elements of the film seem to come together into some kind of shape that unfolds, that refers to itself, and in various other ways "make sense." That is, even if one thinks that these are just random images and sounds (which I don't), they would nonetheless be random images and sounds that cohere in some way such that, for example, it would be surprising if at any point in the film the very next frame was an hour-long, unaltered, high-definition clip from a televised basketball game. And indeed, this logic (for lack of a better word) is part of the process of making a piece—part of Egan's creative practice, to use the term that many artists have adopted.

Years ago, when I used to work at an arts university, I would often ask students to chart how they understood the final ten versions of a piece they were working on to be improvements on one another, and the answers—especially by the best students—were often remarkably obscure. That is, it is a simple thought to imagine Egan working at, for example, getting the placement and pacing of the letters just right, but that thought quickly becomes extremely complex when we start to think about what "just right" specifically means and to query what the earlier versions—which, presumably, were just a little wrong—didn't get right. In short, what are the active forces of rightness in the making of the piece?[6] Often, such conversations with students would edge toward methodological discussions, but this isn't quite right: the particularity of artistic practices—their aesthetic—often bears a vexed relation with methodology, because the latter tends to assume the schematic, informatic model of knowledge that this book has been troubling through the concept of incommunication: a method ultimately in some sense assumes a model whereby knowledge can be developed as a particular instance of a generality and can thus be exchanged (because the preexisting generality crafts a plane of invariance between different particularities). Again, this isn't wrong per se, but there is something about artistic practice that is often, at least in its impulses and motivations, ameth-

Algorithms, Art, and Sonicity   87

odological (especially in the sense of a method as a—usually disciplinarily validated—way of making a claim such that future claims can be made on the basis of its accepted veracity).[7]

In short, there is always a kind of practiced logic to particular things that is not captured in their generality, and this is at once what is specific to the thing and, paradoxically, what it shares. To speak of creative practice in this way is to speak of its incommunications. In the case of *Ransom Notes*, what we are seeing when we see the piece as a piece (as opposed to just as a random succession of images) is precisely this incommunicative logic, even though it obviously is visible to us only insofar as we can't quite articulate or grasp it—because if we could grasp it precisely, that would mean being able to reduce it to its component parts, at which point we wouldn't be taking seriously the qualitative difference between partial and full communication that textures its incommunicative profile. Thus, we could say (succinctly, if a little obscurely) that part of the piece is only available to us through its unavailability. Importantly, this unavailability is also only vicariously available for Egan as well: a lot of planning goes into making a piece like this—there are methods, if not a methodology proper—but ultimately there is a crucial component of the process of making it that can't be explained but can only be known within the actual (if logically ephemeral) process of its making.

To be clear, to insist on this element of knowledge—to insist on knowledge's incommunicative actuality—is not to insist on a hierarchy between making and observing as method, nor to argue for anything like a primacy of authorial intention. One needn't, of course, understand an artist's intentions in order to talk about what they produce; indeed, this applies to artists themselves as well. Instead, I am simply insisting at one and the same time on the necessity of being able to "make" in some sense—physically, conceptually, and otherwise—if one is to discuss that which is made, and on the temporal difference between the implied future of being able to make or remake a piece and the always already of any specific piece that guarantees its absolute singularity.[8] That is, Egan can gain some purchase on her process because she knows in general how to make the works that she has made, but the decision process of actually making is distinct from any account of such a process even for her. Aesthetic activity is always undertaken at a certain remove—and aesthetic activity is involved in all activity (when it is thought incommunicatively).

88   Chapter Four

Part of what this means is that knowledge itself—not just what is known, but what constitutes knowing—is both enacted and contextual in a way that changes over time and according to different places, infrastructures, and so forth. As discussed with Fathead, knowledge is better understood in terms of (not necessarily conscious) decisions that never come from a single origin; decisions that, for their part, are different before, during, and after the moment in which they're made in such a way that the incompatibilities of such differences are revelatory of something in a decision that withdraws from availability. Thus, for example, even Egan doesn't have access to her aesthetic decision making in *Ransom Notes* because it is of a different order than her recollection of it, and this incommunicative (in)coherence is the case at macrohistorical scales, at the scale of individuals, and (as this book emphasizes) at the microscales of digital technologies as well. This is the temporal-scalar incoherence through which, in their incommunicative enaction, worlds continue in their apparent coherence.

In other chapters of this book I have thought through the ways that knowledge is technically specified in the context of digital technoculture. In this chapter, I emphasize the ways that specifically the available unavailability of aesthetics accesses this problematic, not least because "for the first time in our history, media (meaning the storage, dissemination, and transmission of experience) has become distinct from its own technical infrastructure, from the computational networks and machines that undergird most of what we consume as media."[9] This is the singular newness of new media today that is different than its plural antecedents; different, that is, than the way that the novelty of every medium waxes as an incipient innovation before waning into the sedimented form of the medium itself. If so much of our new media involve "technical operations to which humans lack any direct access" and thus take place according to causal logics that are constitutively—constitutively!—beyond human scales of perception, the available unavailability of aesthetics, and the causal and temporal weirdnesses that come with it, is also the enabling condition of digital culture.[10] For me, this suggests that we might be able to listen differently to digital culture by folding it together with aesthetic practices—or rather, by listening to the enfoldments of technicity and aesthetics that are apparent in technoculture's incommunications.

Truthfully, this isn't really much of a stretch. Aesthetic practice is a form of occult decision making and is always caught up in material-

Algorithms, Art, and Sonicity   89

semiotic ecologies. Importantly, though, to ask what an aesthetic practice *is* is slightly different than asking what it does, and, specifically, a crucial part of what an aesthetic practice does is enacted by the term itself: aesthetics (the term) functions rhetorically as a shorthand for the coupling of humans and technics that is always—implicitly and explicitly—part of the ongoing unfolding of a human's worldly experience. In the context of creative practice, then, what connects the myriad undertakings that might be considered aesthetically is a conjecture that creativity is in some important sense technical: one must eschew (or at least supplement) a Romantic perspective understanding creativity as the progeny of an authorial genius in favor of an understanding that avows the role of specific, contingent, machinic processes. To work aesthetically is not simply to offload calculative labor to a conscious decision or even to a medium or to a machine, but rather to meaningfully engage the creative process itself by making explicit the ways that such labor produces the creative insight from which it appears to follow. It is obvious, but bears repeating: human agency does not describe a knowing subject in full possession of themselves who makes use of a passive world that stands as a reserve for the actualization of their desires. Rather, agencies—the plural is important—are more effectively thought in terms of distributed ecologies of patterns, textures, feedback loops, redundancies, and so forth that may or may not subtend the scales and perceptions of human individuals at any given moment.

In this context, the algorithmic composition *Toll* (2012) by California composer Evan Merz is instructive, as Merz's approach to algorithmic composition explicitly engages this paradigm. In *Toll* (and in other works) Merz uses a software program (which he wrote) to cull sounds from the user-contributed database at Freesound (https://freesound.org) and organize them into graphs. He then activates (i.e., plays the sounds of) the graphs by traversing the nodes. Specifically, Merz's program exploits the "aural similarity relationships provided by freesound.org [and the] lexical relationships provided by wordnik.com" in order to produce the graphs, the vertices (i.e., nodes) and edges (i.e., connections) of which can be visualized in the manner we usually associate with depictions of networks.[11] Merz then temporalizes these with a program that moves between vertices according to a specific cellular automaton.[12]

Toll stems from Merz's explicit conception of algorithmic composition as a simulation of creativity. Moreover, Merz works specifically according to a model of cognition developed by Melissa Schilling that describes moments of creative insight as occurring when an atypical association reconfigures a subject's field of representations such that shortcuts are created: creative insight for Schilling is "a process whereby an individual moves suddenly from a state of not knowing how to solve a problem to a state of knowing how to solve it."[13] If we imagine the field of representations through which the problem is articulated as a basic nodes-and-edges network visualization, this process is equivalent to shortening the path length from the problem to the solution. As small-world graph theory has demonstrated, such a shortening is readily accomplished by reconfiguring the field through the addition of random new connections.[14]

It's worth noting that this approach to creative insight is historically specific, and really is part of what might be called a computational *dispositif*, or what Katherine Hayles has diagnosed as the Regime of Computation.[15] That is, we might consider Schilling's approach to creative insight to be computational in that it frames every problem as a quantity of flattened time: as a quantity of labor measured in computing cycles rather than man-hours. In the context of this understanding of a computer—which isn't really incorrect, but which neglects the role of incomputability discussed elsewhere in this book—there is no such thing as a problem proper but rather simply a quantity of computation required to actualize an end that is encoded in the field of possibilities from the beginning. To the extent that a computer is a machine that can compute anything that is computable (given enough time and memory), computing itself does not definitionally change regardless of what is computed. Indeed, the same particular creative— or "creative"—paradigm underwrites contemporary machine learning, in which the meaning of *learning* is taken as a given (i.e., it does not definitionally change) so that what is learned can be tracked, measured, and in this way guaranteed.

Thinking of creative insight computationally is thus a two-step production: it qualifies insights as computable problems, and thus quantifies them in terms of how much computational time and memory they require to solve. In the case of *Toll*, we can see Schilling's approach to creativity reflected in Merz's software if we understand aural similarity as configuring the field of Freesound files at any given moment (i.e., all possible files exist as an expression of their recursive similarity to the source file) and lexical relationships as disrupting and thereby redistributing this field by changing

Algorithms, Art, and Sonicity   91

the source file (i.e., introducing a new node and the potential for creative insight in the form of alternate paths).

However, this raises the question: if we are thinking of *Toll* (or *Ransom Notes*, for that matter) as solving a problem, what precisely is the problem that is being solved? A first answer might just be the production of an artwork, but this response is unsatisfactory for a couple of reasons. First, the piece is clearly indebted to a tradition of Cagean aesthetics wherein the problem of creativity at the level of production is always already solved because anything is potentially interesting. Indeed, Merz's work explicitly recalls in particular Cage's *Williams Mix* (1952), a piece that distributes an "enormous heap of tape fragments [into] six categories . . . [and subjects them to *I Ching* manipulations], producing constant jumps from one sound to another or . . . textures of up to sixteen simultaneous layers."[16] More than just referring to this Cagean aesthetic, *Toll* actually relies on this understanding to be considered a piece in the first place (rather than as just a succession of sounds) since the piece does not employ most of the rhetorical mechanisms that conventionally frame a piece of music. As Steven Connor puts it, musical listening "activates a minor form of . . . hallucination . . . in which we actively give to the sounds we hear a kind of structure and expressive intent that they might otherwise not possess."[17] The artistic tradition *Toll* draws on literally creates the conditions for its (hallucinatory, though by no means unreal) appearance as a piece of music.

Second—and following from the first point—the speculative nature of the Cagean approach means precisely that the aesthetic demand is shifted from needing to satisfy an existing definition of *beauty* to opening a new texture to which we might learn to listen. The beauty is in the listening, and the piece's contribution to this is as much to facilitate a listening away from the determinations by which listening is seduced. That is, in the speculative aesthetics invoked by *Toll*'s creative rhetoric, it is not the problem field that is reconfigured—that is, the distribution of nodes and edges—but rather the very constitution of the nodes and edges within it; the internal inconsistencies of the network's valences, affordances, weights, and so forth.[18] As Anna Munster demonstrates, to take an edge seriously "means to value the force of relation—its capacity to change the things in relation at the very moment change itself relationally occurs."[19]

Put simply, it just isn't compelling to think of the protocols embodied in Merz's software in terms of generating creative insight if the latter means

92   Chapter Four

solving a problem. Anecdotally, this jibes with the experience of most practitioners who, in my experience, would identify what they do as at least partially involved in problem expansion rather than solving: artists typically speak of extending rather than contracting the time between the moment of encounter with a work and the moment when it is folded back into the banality of everyday experience.

Rather than engaging the problematic of a problem, then, we instead might think of *Toll* in terms of sonification, but specifically an incommunicative sonification that takes up both the data set (the Freesound samples) and the algorithm that sounds them. That is, Merz's algorithm sonifies the Freesound database as a selection of aural and lexical similarities, but the piece—that is, the necessarily doubled existence of this technical algorithm as an aesthetic proposition—sonifies the algorithm itself, which is otherwise unavailable. The piece conjures and sustains a field of incommunication in which the virtual and affective activities that constitute aesthetic attention are understood to be themselves productive. The problem of making sense is inverted when it is asked in the arena of an aesthetic proposition: anything works, it is just a matter of finding out how and—if we're interested in engaging its incommunicative field—deciding the extent to which (to paraphrase Bateson) this working is a working that makes a work.

Insofar as this invocation of sonification takes the latter to be an iteratively recombinant aesthetic proposition, the term *sonification* itself becomes a bit of a misnomer. Sonification typically implies a simple medial translation—a relatively neutral case of transcoding—wherein some inaudible information is made audible, perhaps exposing patterns that we might not notice were the information presented visually.[20] Christina Kubisch's "electrical walks"—public walks "with special, sensitive wireless headphones by which the acoustic qualities of aboveground and underground electromagnetic fields become amplified and audible"[21]—are exemplary of this approach in the arts, which in presenting art as "the medium of conveyance for that which we cannot speak" has been criticized (notably by Seth Kim-Cohen, as discussed in chapter 1) for neglecting the "reality that art, as a cultural activity with a tradition and conventions, . . . constitutes and is constituted by a vast meaning-making structure."[22] Put schematically, sonification tends to work by actualizing a potential such that, if one is lucky, a shift in the field of what actions are possible is redrawn; that is, the actualization of potential brings about a secondary shift that takes hold as a new set of possible advances upon the information now audibly sensible.

Listening to *Toll*—and other algorithmic compositions—works differently, though, because it places this secondary virtualization (i.e., the virtualization that comes as an indirect result of sonification's actualizing movement) in contact with the primary virtuality that is aesthetic listening. Virtuality is primary in aesthetic listening because aesthetic listening involves listening in such a way that what one hears at a given moment can and does alter what one has already heard: values and valences are conferred retroactively such that the present is a future that did not exist—even as a possibility—in the past.[23] In this way, algorithmic compositions place the virtuality that characterizes aesthetic listening in a continuous feedback relation with multiple processes of actualization (i.e., the literal sonification that makes up the material of the work) such that the process itself is what is evident. We hear the ongoing incommunicative resonance of this complex field of virtuality, potentiality, and actuality that is continuously productive of performative excesses.

In listening to *Toll*, we are not presented with a sonified pattern of information that just happens to be temporalized, but rather with an ongoing temporal process that, as a result of its ongoingness, affectively entangles listeners in an incommunicative relation. This entanglement is incommunicative in part because to know a feedback loop isn't to be able to offer a kind of blow-by-blow playback of it (e.g., to be able to say that sound x is followed by sound y, and so forth, as such a linear sequence is unintelligible in a feedback system) but rather to hear it in such a way that one can feel from moment to moment the specific ways it could sound different than it does. Following William James, "knowledge is not a project of collecting, analyzing, and categorizing [but is instead] radically pragmatic, 'a world working out an uncertain destiny.'"[24] Listeners become aware of the specific contingencies that are operative in *Toll*'s triangulation of their incommunicative interplay between self and world, and what is exchanged in the process is precisely the inexchangeability of the singular, inarticulable excesses the entanglement catalyzes.

An algorithmic musical composition does not so much solve a problem in the piece that it results in, but rather results in a piece through which we can approach the problem of interacting with the extrasensory algorithmic activities that it performs. A piece like *Toll* isn't an end in itself, but a kind of cipher for algorithmic attunement: it takes extrasensoriality as a topological invariant that allows algorithms and aesthetics to be folded together (i.e., because both are extrasensorial). Indeed, because we can suspend the question of whether it makes sense, it is possible that we can incommunicatively attune—over time—to sense-making practices.

Thought differently, the moment of creative insight in algorithmic composition isn't a moment at all, but rather something that continues after a piece has been completed: a piece is a piece because it is one of many algorithmic pieces that together act as a kind of training ground that, insofar as it involves extending time, isn't so much about insight as learning. The sense of learning invoked here recalls the ultimate fate of the Fathead project as one that is about collective knowledge in its relational dimension: learning means approaching one's body as an "ecology of practices" that is in cocomposition with the environment.[25] Schilling to the contrary, we do not short-circuit an informatic field through a sudden insight into how the piece works, but rather make use of the aestheticized presentation of the algorithm to extend our encounter with it beyond the clock time of the piece. We hold it as a piece such that we too may be held in an incommunicative embrace.

While *Toll* uses algorithms as a tool to think about the interscalar strangeness of algorithmic creativity, then, we are perhaps better served in this endeavor to listen to practices that leverage this aestheticized human-technology coupling rather than isolating a computational process. That is, what might we learn from practices that attune to the unsiteable relationality of human-technology coupling by moving beyond an understanding of technology as an adscititious tool of human development? Exemplary of this approach is Julian Pivato's performance piece *Yesterday Wants More* (2013–14), wherein the artist gives a daily live performance of the Carpenters' song "Yesterday Once More," backward and a cappella. Despite being an a cappella performance, this piece clearly depends on a technical infrastructure for its production in a number of ways. For example, the performance requires extensive practice and preparation that was only possible through the repetitive listening afforded by recording technologies. Moreover, the reversed version of the Carpenters' song is, more specifically, a forward version of the recording played in reverse, a distinction that makes the song inseparable from its techno-material instantiation. And finally, Pivato's first step in learning the piece was to produce a score, itself formed through the technology of writing.

What bears noting in *Yesterday Wants More*, though, is the feedback relation that Pivato's learning process creates between this infrastructure, the aesthetic concerns of the resulting piece, and the myriad material constraints at work: Pivato's embodied activity—which is not to say their body, but rather their entrained bodily activities—attunes these diverse dimensions of the work. And indeed, this draws out the (reiteratively constituted) material concerns that are embedded in the aesthetic proposition of the piece's musicality: as they note, "performed in retrograde, the components of this well-used Carpenters song are loosened, re-calibrated and carefully relearned to satisfy a very different hearing. . . . The musical material—the notes, where to breathe, the rhythm—all these things were more complicated because they were just OFF. Off balance, off rhythm, off."[26]

The point is, *Yesterday Wants More* exemplifies learning as attunement (rather than as data acquisition) because its ongoingness is not about Pivato accurately aping the reversed recording, but rather about placing—dispersing—themself outside of themself (i.e., into the score, the recording, the practice, and so forth) such that they can become the machinic reversal (and vice versa). Pivato catalyzes an incommunicative ecology. Indeed, the process of creating the piece was inseparable from that of learning it and worked in precisely this manner: Pivato proceeded by "working back and forth between score, recording, reversal of recording and score (correction) until [they] got it right. . . . [Working on it daily for several months,] every once in a while [they] would check [themself] by reversing a recording of that day. . . . It was never perfect but it was recognizable."[27] As they point out further, while somewhat accurate mimicry is a concern in this process, it is not an end in itself, which was also the case with respect to the musicality of the resulting performance. Instead, Pivato's aim (in my understanding) was to attune themself to the singularity of the performance, to the specific ways that the performative exceeds the generic. In short, the technical infrastructure, material constraints, individual affective comportment, and broader aesthetic concerns collectively operate in and as a piece so that the creative practice in making *Yesterday Wants More* lies precisely in finding the ways that the aesthetic logic of the piece is already operative in its technology. That is, they are not reverse engineering a mechanical pro-

96   Chapter Four

cess, but rather learning—through a sustained and painstaking incommunicative practice—how to draw out the aesthetic dimension that is always present in such scenarios, but that is suppressed by the seeming fatality of technics: by the way that extracted technical processes tend to appear in technoculture as computational problems that contain their ends in their beginnings, and thereby leave no room for any articulations but the inevitable and exchangeable. In short, the technical infrastructure, material constraints, individual affective comportment, and broader aesthetic concerns collectively operate in and as a piece that retroactively produces the parts of which it is more than the sum.

To reiterate, in *Yesterday Wants More* Pivato works by engaging in an incommunicative process that leverages the constitutive strangeness of aesthetics. We can understand this as an act of listening not so much because they are working with sound per se, but because the particular type of relationality that they develop cannot be reduced to any of its constituent parts and evades any particular moment or site of capture. Moreover, we can collimate this subjective vector of listening to the technical one constituted by the material histories of audio recording, where recordings catalyze a culture of ubiquitous schizophonic listening—that is, where the separation of a recorded sound from its source is accepted without question—that is a precondition for work of this sort.

This incommunicative concatenation of technical and subjective vectors is perfectly exemplified, for me, in the nine-minute 2015 video *Freezing* by Colin Clark, which invites us to listen to its silence rhetorically: for the specific ways that it attunes to the performative incommunications of the technical ecology at work in the video.[28] Depicting, on its surface, the natural landscape of a Georgian Bay winter, *Freezing* works by folding together the disparate temporal processes of video, video processing, time-lapse video, viewing, and the natural environment it depicts such that we can sense the seemingly mutually exclusive agencies of each simultaneously. To this end, the piece combines in various ways short bursts of time-lapse video; long, relatively static real-time shots; long, relatively static time-lapse shots; and ends with a long fade to black. The piece doesn't include any sound until around the five-minute mark, at which time an environmental wind becomes audible; this wind increases in volume in inverse proportion to the decreasing brightness of the fade to black, and the piece ends with approximately ten seconds of black screen accompanied by relatively prominent wind sound.

Like Egan's film and Pivato's performance, *Freezing* works via its distributed processuality (rather than as some sort of composed expression). The incommensurable scales and logics that the piece brings together in its working work because they are never fully brought together except in the aesthetic performativity of their incommunication. To the extent that Clark authors the piece, then, he does so by catalyzing a resonant relation between the disparate temporalizations of its various components. The fade to black that ends the video, fittingly enough, renders the extrasensory digital speeds of the work visible through prominent digital artifacts. Importantly, what we see are not digital processes, but rather artifacts and symptoms of them: the processes are vicariously available, their unavailability itself made available. These artifacts are accompanied and followed by the most prominent sonic section of the piece, which notably represents its purported content (the wind) by conjoining it with the microphone that records it: the wind doesn't sound to our ears the way that it is typically represented through a microphone, but the latter is no less real for this fact. Rather, the wind sound is revelatory of the technicity that is always at once part of sensation and—at the same time—is the parting of sensation from itself, into its incommunicative ecology. By approaching the natural scene, the sound, the video, the human videographer, and us human viewers aesthetically, each of these are revealed in the specific weirdnesses of their technicity.

In this sense, the aesthetic logic of *Freezing* is called forth in its viewing as much as its making: we know at the beginning of the fade to black that a fully darkened screen will be the end point of the process, but we also sense that this knowing is strangely general, unequal to the complexity of the actual process of its coming about. It is, in short, worth watching the video to the end, even if we know the ending. (Spoiler alert: spoilers don't always spoil!) Quite simply, Clark's compositional process is to operationally attune to a register of experience that can never be lived by conscious experience. Indeed, this explains Clark's attraction to high-definition video in much of his work, which stands in contrast to the community of artists with whom he works—including Egan—who privilege analog media. Clark's use of HD might be thought of as an aesthetic extension of E.-J. Marey's aim with his

98   Chapter Four

nineteenth-century photographic gun, which aspired "to develop sensors that possess sensory domains of their own [in order to] inaugurate new, properly technical domains of sensation."[29] As Clark comments, the fade reveals "vision to have been somehow 'insufficient' all along, especially affectively. [But if] the fadeout confirms that we were listening all along, . . . something was entirely missing from that 'listening,' too."[30]

So here again, it makes sense to say that we hear this piece: the sound of the microphone-wind coupling is particularly exemplary of this because it echoes the condition of all sounds, which can never be reduced to a single source. But more broadly, too, if I insisted above on aesthetic practice as a making available of unavailabilities, I would now supplement that claim to say that one might define aesthetic listening (in part) as an attunement to what is availably unavailable. Remembering that any separation of the senses is at best provisional, to listen is to attend to the effects of a reality the cause of which can never be singly determined: the proverbial sound of one hand clapping is not the limit case of sound but its basic enabling condition.

Of all the entries in the 2019 Biennale, Ryoji Ikeda's 2019 sound and video installation *data-verse 1* may on the surface appear most cognate with the topics of this book: in effect, the piece visualizes large data sets (from CERN, NASA, and the Human Genome Project) as patterns of high-definition white characters on a room-size screen, and sonifies this same data in what the catalog describes as a "minimalist electronic soundtrack (that) weaves entrancing layers of white noise." Engaging in the rhetoric of the data sublime, the piece purports to allow "us to grasp the contours of the vast sum of matter and information that populates our environs."[31]

Clearly, this language is problematic, and the piece itself risks both naturalizing information and quantifying matter in precisely the manner that this book contests. In this respect, *data-verse 1* is continuous with Ikeda's broader oeuvre, which has been both scrutinized and lauded for its privileging of raw materials; his audio work, for example, makes extensive use of sine tones (the simplest wave form) and noise spectra, and often works at the thresholds of human hearing (in terms of both frequency and volume).[32] This precise feature bears noting because there is something in the work that skirts around the possibility of being read particularly, and this qualitatively distinguishes it from the techniques of making unavailability available that I've discussed above. That is, there is a distinction between exoticizing data (as, arguably, Ikeda does in *data-verse 1*) and coming to grips with the particularities of its excesses.

To draw out this distinction, consider another sound-intensive work from the 2019 Biennale, Shilpa Gupta's 2017–18 installation *For, in Your Tongue, I Cannot Fit*. Installed in a dimly lit room, the piece consists of an array of one hundred ceiling-suspended microphones that are reverse wired to function as speakers, each of which hangs above a straight metal stand that comes up from the floor and which has a sheet of paper spiked on it. Coming from the speaker/microphones are recordings of spoken or sung verses (in Arabic, Azeri, English, Hindi, and Russian) of "100 poets imprisoned for their work or political positions"; each corresponding printed sheet features one of the texts, "waiting to be read by one and then echoed by a chorus of disembodied voices."[33]

As with *data-verse 1*, Gupta's work risks exoticizing its content: insofar as the voices "might, in turn, include and exclude the listener, depending on which languages they understand," they function in part as a "soundscape" (with all the complications that term brings). And yet, consider the differences between how these works bring their individuals into contact with their unavailabilities: *data-verse 1*—for better and worse—brings all viewers into a more or less identical relationship with the enormity of data. The viewing experience is alienating, in the sense that nothing of one's particularity is brought into contact with the piece: no matter how much one knows about, say, DNA, this knowledge remains disconnected from its representation in the work. By contrast, not only do individuals stand in different relations to Gupta's work based on their knowledge of particular languages, cultural histories, and texts, but the piece itself is changed by the presence of individuals in the aggregate: to experience *For, in Your Tongue, I Cannot Fit* in a setting like the Venice Biennale is to viscerally experience all that is unavailable to one not only in the objectifying universe of (post) representational art, but also in the pragmatic collective relations through which works work.[34]

To speak of sounding art isn't necessarily to speak of art practices that literally make sound: if it is true, as Claude Debussy famously claimed, that "music is the silence between the notes," then this gives us a hint that we might listen for such silences beyond the realm of music entirely. With this in mind, the final artwork I consider in this chapter is one that does not involve any sound, Renée Lear's video installation *Renée Taking a Sip of Water (Human and Video in Motion)* (hereafter RTSW), shown at Trinity Square Video in Toronto (2013) as a companion piece to Lear's super-slow-motion daily practice developed in tandem with fast frame rate video equipment.[35] (Tellingly, a performance of this practice—which includes literal sound—was given as a companion piece to the installation.) The installation is presented on two large television screens mounted beside one another, with each screen featuring multiple iterations of Lear sitting and taking a drink of water (with minor variations); each iteration is a particular combination of Lear's motion speed, the speed at which the video was shot, and the speed at which the video is played back. In essence, Lear combines human movement with the slow and fast frame rates of the video camera and the slow and fast playback times of video editing software. There is also a three-line text on each screen that describes the playback variation currently being shown (e.g., Renée moving in slow motion/videoed at normal speed/played back at normal speed). As the piece moves along, each video works through the various possible combinations of movement/video recording/video playback happening at a slow/normal/fast rate.

As in both Pivato's and Clark's work, Lear explicitly cares less to learn the "truth" about motion than to "experiment with a new kind of motion that is at once human and video."[36] *Renée Taking a Sip of Water* experiments aesthetically with the material-semiotic incommunicativity of its technical operations. Indeed, this is why the particular manner in which RTSW plays out its temporal combinatorics is so striking: rather than simply presenting information—that is, the truth about motion—or even the kinds of translative differences that come with different recording media (or, as discussed above, with conventional sonification processes or data exoticizations), RTSW gives us the strange asymmetries of her human-video assemblage in their own right: the formal weirdness of the piece—and it is a manifestly weird piece—comes about as much in the durational practice of viewing as in the making itself. If part of the charm of processual work in general is the incipient awkwardness that inheres in any translation, this piece palpates that potentiality—that is, the not-yet-undertaken undertaking that calls forth the question of form in the first place—in a manner that precludes the question of a single objective origin in favor of something like a past to come. As with the final fade to black in *Freezing*, we know precisely what is coming and how, but we don't know where it is coming from. In fact, this is why Lear tells us how each variation is made, because there is no risk of us actually understanding this making—except in the most banal sense—unless we were to undertake the process of making ourselves . . . and even then, as discussed with *Ransom Notes*, the temporalities of understanding are different and incommensurable.

Approached differently, we might say that Lear's striving to "become a video" isn't just an aesthetic choice (though it is that too) and isn't just about problematizing the boundary between person and machine, but is most importantly a choice about just how such boundaries are incommunicatively sustained. Because she crafts a register where she, the video recorder, and the video playback are functionally equivalent, Lear perfectly demonstrates the way that a political language of attunement moves (for better and worse) from the distance of criticism—where critique is "always *about* the real, [but] is forever *against* it"[37]—to a kind of bodily affection. Form isn't an enveloping structure in this work, but instead a capacity to entrain. What it means for RTSW to make sense is to become attuned to the tempi and machinations of its specific ecology precisely insofar as these cannot ever be attuned to. *Renée Taking a Sip of Water* textures an incommunicative relation with technical systems that preclude formal understanding.

Thus, it isn't incidental that Lear didn't so much become video as learn to become video, where learning is understood processually and relationally. We can further specify the bodily dimension of this entrainment precisely—and paradoxically—because it is outside of Lear: it is the technical element that is in Lear but not of her, and that sustains the incommunicative incoherence through which she apparently coheres. What it means for Lear to become video is to become—literally—caught up in the latter's tempi and machinations precisely insofar as these point to a technical system that acts through her when she envelops it and envelops her as she acts through it.

What I hope the above readings hint toward is a way of thinking relations outside of the nodes-and-edges network visualization through which I discussed creative insight earlier. I'm motivated in this because I think it moves in the direction of engaging a substantial contemporary challenge that Anna Munster terms "network anaesthesia." With this nomination, Munster takes note of the prominence that the nodes-and-edges-style diagram has gained in describing relations in our era of computer network technologies. With the phrase "network anaesthesia," then, Munster names "a numbing of our perception that turns us away from [networks'] unevenness and from the varying qualities of their relationality."[38] Put simply, virtually every available image of a network is a variation of the nodes-and-edges form, and this form of diagram obscures the specifics of the relations it represents in favor of a generalized notion of interaction. It occludes the aesthetic dimension of relations, and thereby also the worldly incoherence through which history textures incommunication's texturing of history.

It is no accident that this form comes to such prominence in the double context of late global capitalism and the Regime of Computation, both of which describe a milieu in which exchangeability itself is not changed by what is exchanged. In this respect, capital and information are isomorphic and together limn a mediatic form that technically specifies knowledge in our time as sited in relata that not only precede their relations but are also not qualitatively affected by them. Thus, as Munster puts it, "what we have lost . . . is the experience of the edges, the experience of relation."[39] One might say that we've lost the aesthetics of experience, having been seduced instead by the appearance of communication.

This is why taking aesthetic practices seriously offers so much potential, because they make clear that to ask the question of what it is to know something is always historical, and is to enter into a world of multiple temporalities, a world of iteration, archive, memory, potentials—of past futures, future pasts, and implicate presents. What, then, is it to produce these temporalities in new ways but the creative practice of historicizing? We can think films such as Egan's in terms of how they introduce the available unavailabilities of material-semiotic entanglements; think practices such as Pivato's as the development of an affective-technical attunement; think digital videos such as Clark's as methods of entraining ourselves to listen beyond literal sounds to the reflexive strangeness of technical processes; think Ikeda's and Gupta's contributions to the Venice Biennale for the ways they differentiate available unavailabilities; and think practices such as Lear's as methods of entraining ourselves to the imaginative dimension of the seemingly determinist technological unconscious that permeates contemporary capitalist culture. All these thoughts can all help us to meet the challenge of creativity's plurality in its own key, according to its specific rhythms. Such thoughts might also, in turn, help us understand

Algorithms, Art, and Sonicity   103

scholarship that does not directly bear on art as nonetheless engaged in aesthetic practice, which is to say as thinking that should always privilege the strange and specific things that lure and delight attention over any evaluation of explicit utility. To do so is to begin to recognize that what is typically presented as "useful" is the utility of another, fated trajectory, one that obscures the ways that inutility opens onto itself as an incipient future anteriority of greater and more just utilities to come.

5

Listening and Technicity (Once and for All, Again and Again)

While also setting itself to other tasks, this book has thus far explored listening in several stages. Chapter 1 problematized the medium specificity of sound in order to grasp it as a contingent, contextual object of listening. Chapter 2 then proceeded to consider listening in its technical profile, exploring it through pragmatic engagements rather than seeking to define it. Chapter 3 historicized these engagements by parsing the technics of listening with digital technologies through the logic of computation, demonstrating the affordances and constraints of specifically digital audio. And Chapter 4 further expanded this computational technicity in order to draw out some artistic implications of its aesthetic dimensions (and vice versa). In short, the book thus far charts a course from sound to auditory listening to digital auditory listening, ultimately with an aesthetic sensibility. The present chapter returns this last technical listening discussed with respect to computers back to listening that is independent of computers, and indeed often only adjacent to ears at all. Having demonstrated the contemporary technicity of listening in earlier chapters in part by showing how audition is parsed through computation, this chapter takes a postcomputational understanding of audition to develop an expanded concept of listening that emphasizes the strange technical particularities that come about outside of the computer per se.

To take up postcomputational listening in this way is to take up the afterlife of data in a different inflection than what I offered in the introduction. There, I described the afterlife of data as a moment when data continues to have cultural force in the absence of any belief in its veracity. Here, I unwind what we might—echoing the difference between vision and visuality—think of as "datalities" of listening: ways that listening is organized according to the technics of computational data even in the absence of a computer.

There's a twist, however. A central aim of this book is to latch onto the asystematicities that are carried forth in the various doings that make up a seemingly systematic world. Incommunication, after all, names the world's incoherence with itself: it contours multiplicities of the seemingly systematic world that appear in and as this systematicity. The appearance of universal exchangeability is the form through which the opposite arrives. A promise to return postcomputational listening to the broader context of relational pragmatics, then, will not be to simply apply a computational schematic to contexts outside the computer, but rather to work through examples of the (a) systematic, extra-auditory operations of (incommunicational) postcomputational listening that come about through the schematic's appearance itself. To that end, this chapter gives special theoretical attention to the strange powers of adjacency that come with singular, inexchangeable collectivities in order to unfold the relational and multicausal logics of incommunication. In practice, things will get a little fast and loose—but a little rock-chewing on the topic of listening is necessary before we get to the fun and games.

The quotidian distinction between hearing and listening doesn't hold. One might hear tell that hearing refers to the perception of sound, whereas listening refers to the attention given such sounds. But any concerted attention to the distinction itself announces an indistinction between the two that cannot be held in abeyance. Put simply, any account of listening as attention to hearing must attend to the fact that attention itself is caught up in affective processes, relations, forms, and architectures that have nothing to do with its concentrations. Likewise, hearing is never a question of

106   Chapter Five

simply receiving a signal. Just as we know that mind and body are constitutively and primarily inseparable from one another, so too is the raw data of hearing always already cooked in the cauldron of listening—a cauldron that is itself seasoned from the other uses to which that pot is put.

Listening is an (in)attention to a particular incommunicational economy, and this (in)attention in no sense operates in the sole or even privileged mode of conscious thought. The (in)attention of listening is, for example, played out in and as the physiology of the ear itself: on one hand, it is simple enough to understand the transfer of sound energy from the relatively large outer ear to the tiny oval window (which acts as a threshold to the fluid-filled inner ear) as a materially attentive process. That is, the middle ear functions primarily to concentrate—to focus—the pressure exerted by a sound wave onto an eardrum into an area (i.e., the oval window) that is approximately twenty times smaller than it, working like a thumbtack. On the other hand, though, the mechanical coupling through which this takes place is rather more complex because it occurs via not one but three causally successive bones, the interaction of which allows for—or, put less psycho-centrically, causes—various regulatory functions (see figure 5.1).[1] Thus, as one example of many, when the middle ear's stapedius muscle contracts, it reduces the motion of one of the three ossicles (the stapes, which is the innermost bone in the middle ear and typically the smallest bone in a body) in a manner that affects the transfer of some frequencies more than others. (This contraction regularly occurs as an unconscious reflex when one is exposed to loud sounds, thus protecting—though often belatedly, because it is slower than the speed of sound—the relatively delicate structures of the inner ear.) Crucially, *transfer* is here a term of (in)convenience, purposely chosen over *transduction* because the latter, in being slightly more accurate, might seduce one into forgetting that the entire causal chain—in being called forth as such—occludes the incommunication that is in play: the weird, alluring temporalities of the ecology (or really, the ecologicity) to which listening listens. In listening, we know there are transformative comings and goings, but we can't know the direction of the transformations nor specifically what they entail except in and as sonic systematicities that are produced by the relationality of a (beyond human) sound world that defies being diagrammed as signals, senders, and receivers. A stapedius is at once an impediment to the travel of sonic signals and an amplifier of them insofar as they are bootstrapped to an experience of listening.

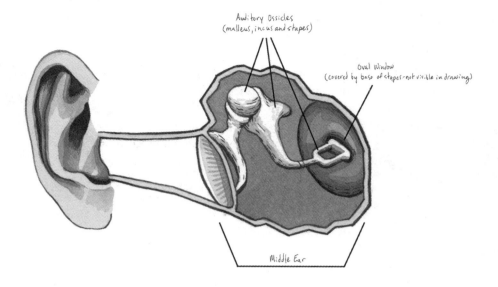

Fig. 5.1. Diagram of middle ear, including auditory ossicles (malleus, incus, and stapes) and oval window (covered by base of stapes—not visible in drawing). Illustration by Luke Painter.

This means that to listen is (among other things) to hallucinate a sound, the reality of which is equally as imaginary as it is physical (though no less real for this fact). We can hear this when we listen to music, for example, which could be characterized as a collective imagination of a type of meaning that is implied by a certain mediation of form.[2] However, emphasizing the hallucinatory dimension of listening is not merely an argument about how hearing becomes semantically meaningful. Listening and hearing are inseparable in part because listening is materially hallucinatory, in that the physical and neurological activities that constitute it do so through processes of filtering, storage, feedback, and transduction that literally require a difference between the gestalt of what is heard (inclusive of the imagination) and any grammatization of it (spectrogrammatic or otherwise).[3]

As a result, insofar as listening involves attention it is equally about misdirections—often material misdirections, and always more than one at a time—as it is about any conventional understanding of focus. In their own ways, musicians will tell you as much, repeating, for example, Debussy's dictum that music is found in the spaces between the notes. Indeed, the challenge of playing in a musical ensemble might be characterized in this way, too: an ensemble setting demands that one listen simultaneously to oneself, to the ensemble as a collective, and to the listenings of the individuals that make up the ensemble (i.e., to what others are listening to and valorizing of the ensemble's activity). In order to play one's part musically, one has to listen away in more than one register simultaneously. To listen collectively is to incommunicate through a recursive and persistent process of (non)selection.

One is caught up in a listening collective when one performs as part of an ensemble. But truthfully, this is the case whether one is performing or not. Insofar as listening is processual, it is always active; and insofar as every sound is more than one, one can't but be caught up in the more-than of listening whenever listening is in play, whether one is listening as part of a musical ensemble, to a (constructed) piece of music, or simply just listening to any sound whatever. In listening, one hears the becoming-collective (or really, becoming collectives) of sounds, and these are never simply found in the sounds themselves. Understood in this way, listening is listening insofar as when one listens, one attends to that of a sound which is not sounded.

Crucially, one listens to these collectives nonlinearly, as systems that output signals that are qualitatively different from their inputs: a sonic collective (i.e., a sound) is a thing of a different sort than its constituent parts (which are themselves secondary to the relational collective). Thus, one listens both to and away: toward that which will always remain apart, and away from the immanent materiality of listening that one can never shake. The sum of all possible attendances is less than its parts, but that less is also (and more importantly) more in that its incommunications proliferate. Sounds have plenty to say, but they don't say it—they say something else.

We listen in part by not listening, then, and we do so as a condition of staying with our incommunicative realities. Listening is "the contraction of all sound, the contraction of all vibrations, which gives sense to sound, contracting clearly just *this* vibration, *this* sound wave, and letting the rest remain obscure, implicated in various degrees of relaxation."[4] And while one might think—in concert with an informatic logic that imagines communication to consist in point-to-point transmissions of data—of this as a simple filtering process, the physiological fact of the matter is that one relies on the dynamism of the middle ear as much as its filtering profile. Put differently, since one hears via the contractively transductive process of audition, and since that process is inseparable from the specific and material misdirections of the middle ear's dynamism (among other dynamisms), it follows that to listen is to attend to the effects of a reality the cause of which can never be singly determined, even as a coming together of more than one. More enigmatically: the proverbial sound of one hand clapping is not the limit case of sound, but rather its basic enabling condition—provided that we accept that every hand is singular precisely because it is itself a multiplicity.

As this suggests, the ecology called forth in listening always includes autonomic and oto-acoustic dimensions, and specifically the ongoing and relentless incommunicative dynamism of intra-ear relations. Thus, while it is true that one breaks a physical transmission in order to have received it, it is more importantly the case that one (materially) conceives a transmission such that one can hear the ongoing relations: the contraction and dilation of the stapedius, in concert with innumerable other processes, the separation of which—that is, the framing of such processes as distinct processes—is always contingent on their systematic appearance. The transductive energetic constellation that allows for questions of meaning(lessness) is dependent on the ear functioning incommunicatively in the form of an alibi, dissimulating its ecologicity in order to function in general even while the particularity of any given instance of "functioning" acts to "disclose [determinable] signals of an otherwise [undeterminable] object world."[5] Listening thus signals sound's (originary) migration beyond its enabling conditions, namely, changes in air pressure. With every contraction of the stapedius muscle, the field of listening expands.

This expanded understanding of sound decenters the role of ears in even technical accounts of listening, which accounts themselves have tended to be deeply and problematically implicated in what Mack Hagood describes as "the objectification of sound that takes place through an enlightenment acoustics of demystification."[6] In reducing auditory perception to signal processing, those accounts have treated hearing according to a strictly mechanistic, objectifying representational logic. While Hagood lucidly critiques such a mechanistic outlook, my point here (as elsewhere in this book, and as Fazi argues with respect to computation) is that even if such a deterministic account were true, signals themselves have ways

110   Chapter Five

of queering their determinations. It's incommunications the whole way down.

The weird indirections of listening scuttle even more strangely as they scale to other physiological dimensions. For example: not a day goes by that I don't consider shaving my teeth. Not "consider" as in rationally calling the question—who still believes that story?—but rather in an etymological sense of the term, the sense in which one pits oneself against a determination of the constellate stars (i.e., [con] sīder-, stem of *sīdus* star). In my consideration, then, I experience the fated paring away of my tooth enamel, and then deny myself the action. (This isn't the most pleasant part of my day.)

This problem started simply enough: when as a youth I bought my first razor, I kept it for a single night in a cup, next to my toothbrush. The first time I picked my toothbrush out of the now shared cup I had to actively select against the razor, which wriggled into my teeth-oriented psyche in precisely this moment of deselection: in choosing to brush my teeth I chose not to shave them, and the bond was thereafter forged. I've long since moved my razor to a separate location—a different drawer altogether. But though the results are hygienically salutary, the experience sticks. A toothbrush is forever a nonrazor in my morning ablutions, and that "non" is experientially parenthetical.

The temporality at work here is worth noting, not least because it is incommunicative: in a very real sense, the I that brushes my teeth is produced after the fact of the impersonal (though pointed) sensation of scraping tooth enamel. It's the only thing that makes the latter bearable: there is nobody who has to bear it, because it exists in the form of a thought that hasn't yet landed on its thinker. To insist on this is not to invoke some kind of caricatured postmodernism that jubilates in displacing the I, but simply to show that such displacements are not in opposition to experience. We can understand this incommunicative truth—as Fazi does—from thinkers such as Whitehead, but we can also under certain conditions feel the weird relationality that such a perspective describes: we can feel a world that flows from a subsequent hallucination of identities (human and otherwise) that are compelled to experience.

The similarities between the nonoccurrence of listening and my unshaved teeth are clear enough: if listening profiles a compulsion toward an

Listening and Technicity (Again and Again)   111

experience that never occurs, the psychedelic adjacency catalyzed by the proximity of my toothbrush and razor to one another likewise indicates an experience that occurs in its nonoccurrence.[7] (Both also describe an experience of the primacy of relations over relata.) Yet transduction and deselection aren't quite the same thing, and the difference is one that matters in this case because to insist on the hallucinatory element of listening is to describe the qualitative difference that comes with scaling. When one listens, one filters down to one's perceptual capacities while simultaneously imagining up to worlds, such that these scales of experience are qualitatively distinct from one another. The I of listening is thereby incommunicatively constituted by the nondialectical relation of these scales, which themselves come about in and as the incoherence of the world with itself. It isn't just, as Bateson says, that "the partial truths of consciousness will be, in aggregate, a distortion of the truth of some larger whole" but also that the whole itself is a distortion of the smaller truths of which it is composed: *large* and *small* are at least as varied as they are invariant with one another.[8]

Since this worldly incoherence is the very meaning of experience, we experience it all the time. Such is the benefit of the term *incommunication*, which names this paradox in its ongoing, pragmatic becomings. While opportunities to explicitly cognize this incoherence are somewhat more rare, one relatively common form of doing so is to listen to one's dreams, specifically as experiences in their own right (rather than, for example, as symptoms). Dreams are fundamentally material and nonabstractable, and we can learn something from them if we focus on their experiential effects rather than merely relating them (symptomatically) to conscious thought. Just as data is the historically specific appearance of the impossibility of communication in contemporary technoculture, dreams bring worldly incoherence to consciousness in ways that are both specific to consciousness and illustrative of its limits.

I recently had a dream that I'd dreamed before. It isn't quite right to say that the dream recurs, since the dream is never exactly the same. I've had recurring dreams, and these weren't those. Instead, these dreams played back into my experience again and again; they recurred the way that singing recurs when it is done in a particular register, at a particular tempo, in a particular style, and to particular ends. The continuities between repe-

112   Chapter Five

titions are real and they matter, but one still has the sensation of singing anew. In short, my dreams did and didn't recur in the same moment of appearance, only truly occurring in this quasi-recurrence.

In the dream, I am in a room that is something between a loft apartment and a warehouse. I'm seated in a heavy wooden chair like the ones my schoolteachers often had, thick with veneer; not the type with metal legs, stretchers, and rails that we students sat in, but the heavy oak kind, with armrests. But I also am not sitting, because I am observing myself sitting in the chair from the vantage of someone who is above and to the side (as in the corner of the ceiling). This vantage implies I'm floating, but I have no such airy sensation.

Looking down and across at myself, there is an old wood-handled shotgun over my knee, balanced by the combined solidity of my and the chair's left arms. The gun is notably large but seems strangely weightless, although I can't really corroborate this levity because—as with my floating self—I don't have a sense of the sitting me as experiencing anything in a bodily way: there is no scent in the room; neither any sounds nor any notably textured silence. The sitting me is wearing blue jeans and a nondescript long-sleeved shirt, but the clothes are just kind of there, in the way that a toenail (ideally) is.

I'm looking downward at myself, my look impassively returned by the sitting me—looking upward at myself, my look impassively returned by the floating me. The calmness of my eyes, sitting in the chair, is most remarkable because of the state of the lower half of my face, which is a mess of flesh, blood, bone, teeth, and hair hanging precipitously in disarray from the sunken remains of my shattered jaw and cheekbones. I've fired the gun into my mouth, it's clear, with devastating consequences.

And yet, neither of me is upset, because we know—in the way of dreams—that the decision to pull the trigger and end our life is somehow one that while materially enacted has also not yet been made. Instead, the scene is one of a resonant question, a funny question (actually) that comes to one of me—I'm not sure which, but I think it's my floating avatar—as one that should by all rights be blithely posted on social media.

"Any friends ever been dead?" the post would read.

"I've shot myself in the face and I'm trying to decide if I should undo the action or just go with it."

In the dream, I feel frustrated by the fact that I don't have my computer with me to write this in the moment (as it were), as well as a certain plaintive resignation to the inevitability of losing this jest to my faulty memory. The absent computer, I suppose in the dream, stands for the absent sensation that comes about with the literally doubled embodiment of the dream. Likewise, the thought of undoing is an echo of a computer's command-Z capacities.[9] At least, that's how one of me interpreted things at the time. The sum of a doubled body is less than its parts, but more so.

Looking down at myself in the dream, I've the acute sense of the decision taking place in the style of a computational interface. That is, the pattern and texture of a decision is given in its meaningfulness—in its eventfulness—but it is given as something distributed, reversible, exchangeable, and ultimately contained: a causal logic that is not properly causal at all. It's more a case of incommunicative empathy, with the sharing distributed to such an extent that it precludes what is shared really being called a feeling. There are nodes of resolution, of course: if unsensed push came to unfelt shove, I would probably reside in the floating me—but the choice would feel arbitrary. Likewise, I am two selves in the dream, but there is always the sense that even this doubled bodily distribution is still something of a concentric force that only barely resists the eccentric magnetic pull of the other objects in the room that would have me as part of them. All of which is to say that the event of the gunshot persistently slides from something experienced as an event to something felt—by whom is not clear—more like a vibration, a sympathetic resonance of the actants in the room: my two selves, the gun, the chair, and indeed time itself palpating in and as the networked affordance that might lead to an event. The decision—the eventfulness of my suicide—is simultaneously "no longer . . . [and also] not yet" taking place, "largely impossible, if also . . . operational."[10]

In short, what might appear as a decision to shoot myself in the face is more properly the incommunicative affordances of the scene—dreamed according to the logic of a computational interface—reinforcing themselves. I feel a sensitivity to what Steven Connor calls resonation: a resonating mimetic interlocution between the proximate actors, human and nonhuman alike.[11] An echolocation of affordances; a locution of inters from which emerges—through the sudden reconfiguration of the field that will have been articulated by the firing of the gun—the incommunicative human-bullet coupling that is the would-be event of my death.

114   Chapter Five

Dreams like mine are real, and experiencing them doesn't just sidestep a waking mind that would insist on linearity, but actually demonstrates the creative elaborations such a mind undertakes in order to ground itself. If dreams offer an experience of, for example, a time-traveling dimension to suicide, then it is waking consciousness that falls short by failing to acknowledge the ways that one is constantly leaping into the past to produce causes of the manifest effects of lived anxieties.[12] Moreover, since one can dream of the experiential couplings of humans and nonhumans alike—of the ways that chairs, guns, denim, and spaces each listen in their ways—it becomes clear that the impossibility of these is a production of waking thought, a dreamed death that is less than the sum of its parts, but more so.

Dreaming, then, incommunicatively figures sensation as something other than signal processing, and can thereby analogously elaborate our attunements to the excesses of sonic experience. Like dreams, sounds particularize in individual bodies such that they occupy the material space through which those bodies relate, which is to say the intervals, tempos, intensities, amplitudes, contours, and boundaries through which they become bodies in the first place. A dream makes no demands except to be dreamed, just as a sound makes no demand but to be heard. Acknowledging this not only poses a problem for communication, but in fact is the problematic form of communication itself: the form through which an informatic paradigm wherein relations are mere connections—indifferent to their content, and qualitatively equivalent—is denaturalized. And from this denaturalization it becomes clear that to listen is to dream the effects of a reality the cause of which can never be singly determined, even as a coming together of more than one: again, the proverbial sound of one hand clapping is not the limit case of sound, but rather its basic enabling condition—provided that we accept that every singular hand is itself a multiplicity. A sound is less than the sum of its parts, but more so.

As I hope is clear, to figure listening and sound as dreaming is to insist on their technicity. This technicity is contemporary, contoured according to the hegemonic incommunicative aesthetic of computation, even though it has nothing to do with computers per se. This isn't particularly surprising: there has been ample scholarly insistence on both the embodied status of media and the body's status as media. Less attention, though, has been paid to the ways that bodies embody the media of their time. In the case of the

Listening and Technicity (Again and Again)   115

present historical moment, computation notably inflects contemporary culture both in the technical particularities I've discussed throughout this book and in the computer's status as a fundamentally convergent medium. Computers don't just introduce a particular, universalizing exchangeability, but also embody this exchangeability in their status as multi-, meta-, and postmedial devices. This can lead our embodiments of them to appear strange indeed.

During a training session, my squash coach once admonished me for not feeling the rhythm of the game. I knew exactly what he meant. Squash is, unlike many other sports, centered on the movements of a ball in a space that is physically confined. One way to think about tennis, by contrast, is as a competition focused on expanding one's opponent's court while contracting one's own: players routinely play tennis from outside the lines of the court with a mind to moving within. The court is the arterial system of tennis; the game play is the expansion and contraction that comes with pressure modulations applied in specific places with specific intensities, timings, speeds, and durations.

This is not the case with squash, and the result is that in the sport's perfect form the squash ball isn't so much sent back by a player's racquet (as it is in tennis) as it is rejuvenated; the ball is made young again, its possible futures multiplied in terms of both its energy and the potential paths it might travel. That is the job of the player: to give something of their youth to the ball, such that the creative exploits of its motion might continue. To play in rhythm thus requires, first, that one become fluid to the transient channels that infold and ingress the sport's confined context. That is, squash isn't just a general interactive form, but is rather a complex situation of transductive relational recursions in which power plays can only flow from tactical plays that are tuned in to the resonant frequencies of the specific situation, and specifically tuned in to the qualitative differences (between the player's and ball's youthfulness, for instance) that make transduction possible. I wasn't tuning in to that.

There is a second element of playing in rhythm that follows from this, namely, the demand to feel what the ball wants and to respond to those wants with sophistication and sensitivity. To feel in this way—to listen to the squash ball—is to work incommunicatively, because the relation is secured precisely through the impossibility of its actually taking place. The appearance of communication—in this case felt—is nonetheless crucial:

one can't excel on a squash court without in some sense opening oneself to the particularities of each given moment that comes to pass through the generalities of the sport, even as they only come to pass as particularities—that is, in their actuality—by differentiating themselves from those same generalities. One can listen to this paradox as the demands of the ball, even (and only) if they are never spoken or heard as such.[13]

Even if each is its own thing, one can still observe different types of balls. The squash court seems to attract balls of a sort whose personalities demand a constant, cyclical flexion: initially, the ball requires energy and attention in inverse proportion to proximity, such that one runs toward it with steps that gradually slow into a lunge as one draws closer only to, at the moment of contact, have the polarity suddenly switch such that one is shot in the other direction, away from the ball and back toward the center of the court. The ball procures our attention like a certain kind of lover might: "Hurry to me, come to me, slow down and be with me, get the fuck away from me, don't go so far—I miss you, hurry to me, come to me, slow down and be with me." Really, though, the point is more an ethological one than anything else: this form of address is also common to cats, friends, artworks, ideas, computers, chairs, and so forth, each of which at times beckons us to attune in this way. Squash balls, then, didn't invent the loving attunement they procure; they are just constantly in the midst of a rhythmic, instaurating reinvention of it in and for each moment of (incommunicative) courtship.

After admonishing me for "running and hitting the ball" rather than acting responsively, my squash coach offered an instructive media theoretical analysis: because few people in North America grow up watching squash on television, he said, it is much harder for us to feel precisely what the ball wants of our bodies. Even though I've played for twenty years, he was telling me my play lacks historical perspective. Indeed, I lack something of the historical because I am too much in my perspective, which is to say that I am too much in that form of embodiment that I feel as mine when I deny the originary technicity that ensures my embodiment as mine only insofar as I am not isomorphic with myself. In the moment, as I stood spent on the court in physical exhaustion, it was a lot to think about—but the antidote was simple, at least: watch some classic squash matches on YouTube, my coach suggested.

This made sense to me. I've long argued that what can only be called the creative genius of the basketball player LeBron James is to catalyze the par-

Listening and Technicity (Again and Again)   117

ticular affordances that come with being part of a generation that grew up watching hoops on TV. Put simply, James has fully internalized the tele of the television camera—he sees at one and the same time from the bird's-eye vision-at-a-distance of TV and from the eyes on his face. His manifest physical, proprioceptive, and intellectual capabilities are in a real sense in service of this dual vision: while many of his less sensitive contemporaries play in a rhythm that unfurls from the demands of the basketball (as I've described with my squash playing), James plays almost always in three rhythms at once: he responds to the ball's particular form of elasticity on the ground (as it were); he also, though, feels what the camera wants in its more expansive perspectives (both in real time and in its capacity as a recording instrument that will order otherwise only tenuously connected events); and, maybe most remarkably, he hears something of an oscillation between these two experiences that comes about because they are, ultimately, not so much different perspectives as different worlds: different systems that relate to one another complexly and nonlinearly, each with its own unique logics, tempos, actors, and porosities. James plays incommunicatively. In so doing, he literally embodies the mediation of basketball by the future anterior of its recording; or rather, by an implicate present that is felt as the infolding of future and past that is recording's future anteriority playing basketball. This is what my squash coach wanted me to understand, I think.

Of course, there's something else going on in basketball that is different from squash in that it is a team sport, a sport where the collectivity of the game play includes subcollectivities that each involve more than one human actor. In this respect, James's multiscalar perception bespeaks his ability to be receptive to the autopoiesis that is the game, and particularly to the fact that autopoiesis requires poiesis and not just auto-organization. Somehow, autopoiesis requires aesthetic receptivity in order to take place as such, and this receptivity is certainly a gift that James possesses. In the context of a basketball team, though, more than simply being receptive, James is a key agent in a system that also incommunicates such receptivity, internally. Responsiveness in a team context, then, bears not just on the question of players' individual attunements, but also on the question of how the collectivity performatively enacts communication itself in its fully paradoxical, incommunicative, world-disclosing specificity.

To be clear, the communication in play here is (echoing Heidegger, unfortunately) "never anything like a transportation of experiences . . . from the interior of one subject into the interior of another" but is rather the interpretive articulation of "thrownness" into a world together with others.[14] Communication is thus an alibi of poiesis: the primary poiesis of the basketball game produces myriad secondary systems that operate communicatively. Although it is the opposite, too: one can only insist that poiesis precedes communication to the extent that one accepts that alibis are not superfluous, but work instead according to the weird multidirectional causality of supplements. This could be the creed of incommunication: poiesis precedes communication precisely to the extent that communication is prior to poiesis.

It is because the poiesis of the game—which is, remember, inclusive of its mediations and receptions, its histories and its futures—is immanent to the incommunicative operations that lend it internal consistencies that James can hear the part of basketball that takes place on the court systematically. A given moment in a game is, like a murmuration of starlings, a system on the edge, ready to be completely transformed in an instant. James's cyborg televisual capacities thus allow him to adopt a position analogous to that of the scientist who sees a murmuration as a phase transition. The phase transition is possible because everything is connected, but also because there is something that isn't (namely, the observing scientist in the case of starlings, and James's televisual and oscillatory embodiments in the case at hand).

Crucially, though, these other embodiments are not secondary or tertiary ones. The game does not simply emanate outward from the events on the hardwood court, because James's and the teams' responsivenesses—the plural is awkward but important—come about in part as recording's future anteriority playing basketball. This is important because recording too has its murmuring destinies, its aphasic transitions: recording doesn't just seduce the world with its future anteriorities, but is also itself lured by the possible trajectories that unfold from the infolding of these. Television affectively primed James's generation of players to its perceptual apparatuses, entraining a certain mode of ocular listening on the court. However, television too is affectively primed by the bearings through which it is adopted as part of the scalar incommunication that feeds it back to itself as sport.

Thus, the GIF; the short, looping videos that have become such a prominent format for sharing sports highlights.[15] In its capacities for entrainment, the premediation of recording technology fulfills its murmuring destiny in the GIF's looped rhythms. The GIF is television's entrainment

Listening and Technicity (Again and Again)   119

entrained by its entraining having always been in touch with something else, something aesthetic that binds it together in lived incommunications that are the simultaneous before and after of its world disclosures. These entrainment capacities include, of course, not just the players but also us ocular listeners who hear a GIF's rhythms with our eyes.[16] In the future anterior of the GIF's priming capacity, one must already have been receptive and responsive in order to move toward those same frequencies.

Indeed, this fate loops back to another squash experience: during a match, my opponent—an eleven-year-old aspiring member of the Canadian Junior National Team—placed a video camera above the court so as to record our match. It was a GoPro. His favorite feature about it? That it can smoothly and easily edit videos for social media. "I love sharing this stuff with my friends!" he exclaimed in youthful exuberance, before adding, "And it's perfect for GIFs, too."

Of course, while the GIF is a fate of recording technology, it is not the only one: fate's saving grace, as it were, is that it is always more than one. And while LeBron James is a singular site of creative basketballic invention, he too is not the only one: while James's multiplicitous (tele)visuality allows him to catalyze collaborative craftings of new possibilities, we might listen to the courtly genius of a different player, Stephen Curry, for a different media genealogy.

I've suggested that basketball GIFs embody a will to loop that gestates in playing-recording couplings. Basketball video games unfold a different will in this coupling, what we might think of as the television camera's visuality, which is to say the contexts and interactions that the camera and its televisual apparatus potentially capture. Of course, in such an understanding the camera functions equally well—and in many respects better—in its actual absence, such that it does not so much capture as constellate: a "cameratic" aesthetic gets fully fleshed out through the angles, cuts, divisions, and focal points that only become possible when light-reflecting lenses are replaced by animation technologies. Hence, the camera completes itself in its obsolescence, an obsolescence that in this case appears specifically in the simulational aesthetic reality of basketball video games.

This is a complex claim, but it is also just basically and pragmatically the case. Any number of athletes have commented in recent years on various feedback relations between their video game and fleshly selves, and

120   Chapter Five

many have also attested to trying player combinations, moves, tempi, styles, and so forth out initially in a video game. Moreover, players express frustration when their video game selves, played by themselves, inadequately execute maneuvers or stylistic elaborations of which their actual bodies are capable. Finally, the most popular basketball game franchise (*NBA 2K*) updates player attributes and capabilities in response to developments in the offline season, so that there is a classic simulational recursiveness in play: players' rankings in the game are affected by their play on the court, which in turn is affected by the results of their gaming in the game, which in turn opens new affordances for gaming the court. The video game's artificiality is, frankly, natural. Simply put, in playing both basketball and basketball video games, players embody Munster's concept of "informatic affect" (discussed in chapter 2), living through the doublings and differentials of the qualitative differences that their bodies incommunicatively enact in and as their implication in circuits that include digital nodes. Video games create players as aggregates of measurable skill values for things like shooting, dribbling, court awareness, and so forth, with each value ranging from 1 to 99 (never 0 or 100, in a nod to the incomputability of infinitude). Today's players can feel these values in their actual game play, both in themselves and also as sites of topological invariance with the myriad biometrics that come with professional athletics.

We can think this a little less obviously, though, by asking what it is that video games want; what does a video game do when it plays basketball?[17] This is where Stephen Curry is instructive, in that he's a video game's dream come true. One of Curry's foremost contributions to basketball was to reinterpret the three-point line on the court. The three-point line technically marks a minimum distance from which baskets are worth three points rather than two, but in practice this threshold had historically been treated as an area: players almost invariably would shoot the ball from just barely behind the line—far enough away to be worth the extra point, but also as close as possible while still being worth the extra point. For Curry—and now for many members of the generation of shooters after him—the latter part of that arrangement has become less relevant, such that he is almost as likely to hoist shots from three or more feet behind the arc as he is from its edge.

This respatialization of the court dramatically impacts the ongoing autopoietically responsive collectivities of the game—the game's incommunicatively driven cultivation of fruitful activities in evolving communities—in ways that are analogous to the phase transitions catalyzed by James's televisuality, not least because Curry's gravitational pull puts enormous stress on any of the game's collectivities that lack the elasticity necessary to incorporate it. Such collectivities include not only the surface tensions of inter- and intrateam (in)communicative structures but also the broadcasting apparatus, which must adopt increasingly wide camera angles in order to stay with the trouble. Not incidentally, these necessitated wider camera angles go against a tendency across televised sports toward increasingly narrow frames that fetishize an individual player's athleticism.[18] Because Curry (following James) has incorporated the televisual perspectives into his individual perception, he hears the camera's blind spots as sites of potential exploit.

Curry and the not-actually-existent camera of the video game play together in slightly different ways, combining the wider camera angles necessary for game play with the explicit, adjustable values attached to specific skills I mentioned earlier: because the video game reads Curry as an aggregate of measurable values, game play amounts to experimentations with combinations of different intensities of the same attributes. This is undertaken with an ear bent especially toward previously inaudible creative timbres that might be indicative of incipient transition points where quantitative differences become qualitative ones—such as, for example, when a shooter is so accurate from such long range that everything about the game play on the court is changed except the mechanics of shooting.

Watching Stephen Curry play basketball can feel like watching a video game. I expect that's the case for him, too. Because he can feel the informaticism of his body, the difference between being a highly skilled shooter and a level-99 shooter becomes perceptible in their simultaneous enaction: basketball becomes at once a game of experimentation with fixed attributes and exactly the opposite, namely, the fundamentally unattributable play of aesthetics.

Actually, this transmedial doubling of experimental vectors is also evident in squash. For example, my precocious eleven-year-old opponent has a habit of winning rallies by hitting a strange shot that bounces off three walls, acutely calling forth the containedness of the court by pinging its contours. When I spoke with him about it, he said he thought of it one day when he was playing a first-person shooter video game in which he ric-

122   Chapter Five

ocheted a simulated grenade around two corners in one throw. Now, the shot in squash is one that many folks do for kicks, but for most players it is a bad (if playful) habit; by contrast, it is a winning one for my opponent (when playing against me), not least because he executes it with incredible precision. And hence, I can't help but think that in hitting it he attunes precisely to the aesthetic of the video game to play it as squash; he attunes to that of the cameratic visuality that is brought forth in the video game in absolute unrepeatability. Or rather, he, the video game, the court, the ball, the YouTube videos, and the sociality of our competitive relationship collectively complete an incommunicative circuit that intensifies a certain quality of attunement once and for all, but also again and again, in a never-quite-possible multiverse of actualities that is nonetheless fated.

POSTSCRIPT

Epidemiological Afterlives

As I write this postscript it is the spring of 2020 and we are fully in the midst of a global pandemic. Maybe, for once, the term *we* is actually the right one, even if the singular articles attached to *midst* and *pandemic* don't capture the massively diverse ways in which people are caught up. The novel coronavirus is a truly global phenomenon, with individuals, communities, and nations alike adopting postures in relation to the distributions of its powers and potentials. Like climate change before (and after) it, the virus—if not COVID-19, the ferocious disease it causes—moves at scales and speeds that evade individual apprehension, so that we mostly feel it through its measures.

As a result, epidemiology is the news of the day, every day, and it is spoken almost exclusively in the language of data. On the surface, these measurements ground disagreements about their believability: debates rage in all corners about how best to respond to the crisis at hand, and these are almost exclusively structured around contests about what it is that is actually happening. There is, of course, the obvious example of a divide between those who do and don't believe in the seriousness of the virus, citing regional differences, testing rates and results, mortality rates, comorbidities, and so forth. But there are also debates whose data-centricity is more subtle: advocates for returning to work mostly don't, for example, come right out and say that they are willing to let vulnerable folks die to protect their profits, but instead argue that any calculus of the health costs of the virus itself have to be weighed against the health costs that come with losing the means to financially support oneself. (The weighing against—rather than in tandem with—here is crucial, because it situates the health costs of lost work as a result of the novel coronavirus, rather than acknowledging that the precarity with which so many people live fundamentally results from the viral contagion of white, patriarchal capitalism's exploitative movements.) Whether it is invoked or not, data is at the center of these debates and their ilk, and the debates are specifically about data's believability.

It is because we can't but believe in the pandemic as a global crisis that we can't possibly believe in the data that would determine it. So there is a deeper disbelief that is evidenced in these debates and that is present in data believers and disbelievers alike. Since epidemiological modeling didn't start with the discovery of the novel coronavirus, it is worth noting that if the data that drives our models could predict the future, then we would not have been surprised by this pandemic in the first place.[1] As Wendy Chun notes (with respect to climate change models), such "predictive models are produced so that if they are persuasive . . . then what they predict will not come about."[2] Knowledge of this fact amounts to an active disbelief in the determinism of facts. This disbelief isn't something extraneous to predictive modeling, but is instead necessary: to the extent that the pandemic demands that individually scaled perception of the phenomenon be wed to its global spread, it also demands both disbelief in one's senses and, in order to maintain a sense of agency, some indistinction built into the data. That is, disbelief in the data—disbelief in both data's universal exchangeability and its limitless accuracy—is a prime driver of the exceptionalisms that are a necessary component of experiencing the pandemic. Whether one feels immune, vulnerable, agential, or otherwise, the fact of any individual feeling misapprehends the nature of the crisis.

More broadly, I would suggest that none of us really believe the datafied predictions of the coronavirus's myriad impacts in any case. How could we, when so many of those predictions contradict one another in so many ways? Perhaps more than ever, we know in our bones that the available information is incomplete, incoherent, and in service of a privileged few, even as we cling to the prescriptions that are uttered as the facts of whatever reality principle we favor. The datalogical future is always also political, biological, affective, aesthetic, racialized, and other things altogether, often in ways that contradict one another. If that is the case, then during this global pandemic we are living in the afterlife of specifically epidemiological data: epidemiology is contouring futurities that structure our daily lives to an unprecedented extent, even if we know they aren't true.

Our most intimate subjective feelings are inseparable from their hormonal and neurological correlates, themselves proxies for Eurological histories of subjectivity that enact something beyond what they speak. Moreover, whenever the song of history is sung, it is always done in ensemble, so that the oft-remarked dispossessions of modern subjectivity—be they unconscious motives, alienating labors, stolen lands and lineages, animating animalities, or otherwise—are themselves distributions of subjectivity: the scientific, spiritual, historical, political, and philosophical ways through which subjects are collectives that think, feel, and act together. If this is the lesson of modern alienation, the novel coronavirus is its completion along at least three trajectories. First, the virus is (factually) accessible (again, as a virus rather than as a disease) only through alienated knowledge techniques, rendering an acutely singular phenomenon as though it were an abstraction exchangeable with others (this is why so many people so much wanted to compare it to the flu, at first). Second, it has resulted in a global alienation of individuals from the on-the-ground contingencies of our communities, distributing us instead (if we're fortunate) through hegemonic, flattening screen technologies. Finally, the pandemic is all the while teaching us to live our disbeliefs in unprecedentedly active ways: hardly anyone purports to know what the hell is happening with all of this, but every step of the way we embody our disbeliefs actively—some by performing social distancing and mask wearing, others by organizing back-to-work protests.

Because I was in contact with potential virus carriers, I've not left my urban apartment in Toronto for twelve days except to walk down the hall to the garbage chute. In a couple days I'll take a trip to the grocery store, but it will be much, much longer before my social routines return to anything like they were. For me—and for many like me who are privileged enough that sheltering in place is a possibility—the computationally informatic figuring of communication has become almost fully literalized. Nearly all of

126 Postscript

my intersubjective activities are collapsed into the metamedial interface of my computers (including my smartphone).

Of course, what becomes obvious with this situation is what was obvious all along: it may well be screens all around, but it isn't screens all the way down. Even having doubled down on the cultural understanding of communication as information exchange, there are otherwise possibilities that remain in play. When I speak with my mother, I'm not really getting caught up on all the family news—there isn't any, after all—so much as I'm performing my part in the bond of our relation. Likewise, for those of us who work in universities the distinction between instrumental knowledge and something like mentorship has never been felt more strongly. Whether on the line with a loved one or in a Zoom room with students, the information we share is an alibi for the sharing itself, itself an alibi for something else—a being-with that is also a more-than, once and for all and again and again.

Communication is never just communication, and it especially is never simply a secondary function of communicants. That story is part of the story of this book, namely, that schemas never fully schematize and that relations precede relata (even if the opposite is also true). We only share insofar as we are taken up in sharings—and the technics through which we negotiate these are historically and culturally specific, material-semiotic, and aesthetic. There is always something else in the mix and, above all else, this book—through the concept of incommunication—listens for and with the singular elaborations that come about in tandem with the reductive exchange paradigm of communication through which computers enculturate. If computers "seek to [reduce] the future to the past," futures nonetheless proliferate.[3]

So it is fitting that I am finishing this book with so many of my friendships, intimacies, and solidarities channeled through relentlessly dull, reductive, and wearying corporate network interfaces—my calendar chock-full of Zoom, Skype, Google, and Microsoft meetings. These render relations boringly literal and often literally boring, and I am far from alone in this lonesome sentiment. But equally apt, people are palpating the indeterminacies of their relations in new ways: intersubjectively through minor variations like video backgrounds and vocal modulations, but also interorganismically through the various practices of fermenting, baking, interspecies companioning, gardening, and so on, of which one sees evidence everywhere from social media to parks to the paucity of requisite supplies in grocery stores. Overwhelmingly, the comportment through which these relations are taken up is, to my ears, incommunicative, and often in extracomputational ways. To be clear, this is not to make a silver-lining argument but to acknowledge the reconfigurations that make contingent fields of relations newly palpable: as our individual isolations intensify, their reversal potentials proliferate in and as new collectivities, and they do so weirdly.

For me—and this directly relates to this book—this has been most prominent in and as a return to musical practice, albeit of a new type. Without belaboring the tale, my training (in a previous life) has left me with a long-standing vexed relationship with music. On one hand, I despise the Euro-centric, masculinist, colonial values that underwrote my classical musical education; at the same time, though, I can never quite shake that education to just enjoy all of the colors of the musical rainbow. As a result, for the past fifteen years or so I've glibly identified as a quasi-practicing nonmusician, and truth be told, I've been entirely nonpracticing for long stretches.

Back in the early 2000s, one of my musical exit strategies was a technically innovative network music collaboration with William Brent.[4] William's musical background resembles my own (though he has remained closer to that world as a professor of audio technology), and we share a general uneasiness about all things musical, even as we can't ever quite quit it. In many ways, this has sustained our friendship, which has lasted more than twenty years despite our living in different countries. In the way of such friendships, the frequency of our telecommunication with one another ebbs and flows, with months sometimes passing without contact, followed by periods of daily exchanges.

I mention all this because the musical practice I've undertaken while in social isolation is a network music collaboration with William.[5] Notably, the collaboration uses so-called bytebeat algorithms as the foundation of its sound, and involves responding in tandem to the audio output of inscrutable algorithms rather than working expressively. That is, all of the audio is generated by the output of simple arithmetic formulas determining each sample in the digital signal thousands of times per second. The primary input to these formulas is a constantly increasing time value, but each formula has a different number of additional parameters that we can freely change to directly affect the signal. Together, these changing inputs determine the raw sample values of the digital audio signal; in other words, values between -1.0 and +1.0. The range of possible values between those bounds is determined by the bit depth as we change it. Our role as (quasi-practicing non)musicians is to control the values of the parameters other than time, as well as the bit depth (i.e., the resolution of a given audio sample value) at which the outputs are read. This is hugely unruly, given the unspeakably complex recursions and speeds in play: the adjustments we make are highly unpredictable, often unrepeatable, and usually result in textures that are fleeting. The audible output is, for the most part, literally noisy, though it can also sometimes resemble the patterns that are characteristic of early video game consoles (such as the eight-bit Nintendo Entertainment System).[6]

There are lots of artful ways that we collaborate in this environment, and many of the tweaks that we've made as our collective practice has developed pertain as much to our musical relationship to one another as they do to the algorithms. (We can, for example, at any time clone the other person's active algorithm and values, so as to—at least partially and momentarily—match audio textures.) Ours is a specifically musical friendship these days, and as in all friendships we continually, dynamically, and recursively elaborate that friendship into forms that will have been there all along: in this case, the literally unimaginable music that conditions and comes from our coming together will have been what we wanted (or didn't want) to hear from the beginning.

We are playing music incommunicatively, and in so doing incommunicating our musical friendship. Despite having spent many hours collaborating in this way, we speak very little during rehearsals and almost not at all outside of them. Indeed, the technical setup constrains vocal communication, since our remote physical locations complicate microphone routing. Moreover, the open-source sound server—JACK[7]—that enables the informatic exchange through which we incommunicate makes extensive speaking during rehearsals unwieldly. For us, in this setting, the music has to suffice; it doesn't, but it does transduce our friendship—which itself transduces the music—in other ways that I can't quite explain. It does so data-phasically. Through an impossibility of communication that takes place under the sign of computational data exchange, we newly incommunicate.

This practice is a reversal potential of data exchange as communication, then. However, it also works by intensifying the energetics of the

Postscript   129

global pandemic to a point of qualitative change. Like many folks, I've felt dramatically and existentially unmotivated since the pandemic began, almost completely bereft of the ability to be productive. This collaboration leverages that affect: since the algorithms are processed so quickly and relentlessly by our computers, the most effective musical strategies often involve lying back and listening to the computer's output. This conjures a host of platitudes about listening that will be familiar to improvising musicians: we sometimes listen with rather than to (the algorithms); we sometimes listen for the activity implicit in inactivity; we sometimes listen together for sums that are more than their parts; and we sometimes listen dialogically in order to source voices to origins other than individuals. For me, this doesn't even feel so much like the much-lauded active listening I was trained in—there is often too much going on to track, anyway—so much as a kind of resigned listening that, magically, relieves my general sense of resignation. So as they play out now, these clichéd modes of listening (or really, of narrating listening) feel different. For the first time (for me), I can sense them as a minor genealogy for the present geopolitical moment. I can feel them as preparatory for a moment when the technique of communication would be so profoundly informationalized that the aesthetic excesses of that form can be felt. The pretense of communication finally (if only momentarily) lifts.

Truthfully, I don't know what this all means. Worlds—so many, in so many ways—are burning. It remains beyond me to really believe that this practice matters in any consequential way, or even that my enjoyment of it is worth noting. But I do know—in the way one does—that something is afoot in this practice. Whatever it is, it speaks in the language of data about actions that act in and as other ecologies altogether, and that do so weirdly, singularly, and relationally in the crevices of the schemas that would seek to capture them.

APPENDIX

Aural Incommunications Seminar Prompt

(To Be Modified and Circulated to Participants)

PROMPT: Start by cupping your hands behind your ears, pushing the outer cartilage rim of the upper parts of your ears forward. Enjoy the directional microphones you've just created for yourself. Things should sound different than before your hands were there, and this different sounding likely feels different too. Take note of this different feeling, this feeling of a difference, and keep it in mind as we proceed.

PRECIS: This will not be a workshop about auditory prostheses. We will, however, take up the opportunity to (each differently) exaggerate the technicity of our hearing in order to think about knowledge relationally and technically.

To wit: we will each wear different auditory prostheses during a seminar in order to leverage our individually different experiences toward a collective one; we will latch the seminar discussion onto the content of a short text, [INSERT TITLE HERE]; and we will enjoy our seminar by tuning in to the ways that latches become levers (and vice versa, and again and again), such that to identify an active element of the seminar (e.g., a person, position, technology, idea, or otherwise) is to modulate it.[1]

---

1. This seminar works best with relatively short, theoretically challenging texts (for example, the final chapter of this book).

Necessarily, some of our time will be spent sharing, fine-tuning, and discussing our prostheses, but the bulk of our time will focus on mining these for the possibilities that come specifically with us all having them together.

Preparations

1. Please read our anchoring text in advance, and bring a print copy to the seminar. The text in question is available via the URL below; it is relatively short (four thousand words), so we should have time to discuss it in as much detail as we like.
2. Please also arrive with some sort of wearable auditory prosthesis. These needn't be perfect objects or completed artworks, as we will begin our time together sharing them, discussing them, and even tweaking; that said, our time will be most fruitful if we all start with something that is already on hand.

In making these prototypes, please remember the prompt above and work in whatever way suits you best. Some suggestions to work from (or even, if you like, simply steal and make for yourself), depending on how you like to work:

- **DIGITAL:** Simulate (in a very specific way) how things would sound if your head were a thousand feet wide. You can do this any number of ways, one of which is to use an iPod, the open-source softwares Mob-MuPlat and PureData, and a set of (preferably noise-canceling) headphones. Some (very simple) code for this is available at the URL below, in case you would like to use or modify it.

- **ELECTRONIC:** Listen from your feet. You can do this by connecting microphones (you can easily build binaural ones from instructions linked below) to audio output through headphones in whatever way you usually do, except also fix the microphones to your shoes, ankles, or otherwise (NB: it is also fun to attach microphones to your hands).

- **PHYSICAL:** Reverse your stereo field by cupping an insulated funnel to each ear, and then routing (maybe using toilet rolls or plastic) the funnel to one on the other side. Or affix glass jars with pebbles (or insects, with holes for breathing) inside your ears, to experiment with listening to multiple auditory horizons simultaneously.

To be clear on two points: (1) these are just suggestions to give a sense of possibilities, so feel free to do what you like; and (2) if you really can't think of anything right now, feel free to just do one of these suggestions. Again, the emphasis will be on collective interactions (under the alibi of discussing the text), not on the prostheses themselves (though, inevitably, the inverse will in some sense be true!).

By all means, feel free to send me an email if you've any questions, queries, or just want to say hello.

Links

- [TITLE OF TEXT]: link to a text of your choice

- Fathead code: http://www.davidcecchetto.net/downloads/Fathead.zip

- DIY binaural microphones: https://www.musicworks.ca/diy/how-make-binaural-microphones

NOTES

Introduction

1 Dutilh Novaes, *Formal Languages in Logic*, 25.

2 Brouwer, *Collected Works*, vol. 1, 94.

3 Harney and Moten, *The Undercommons*, 18.

4 Peters, *Speaking into the Air*, 1, emphasis added.

5 Peters, *Speaking into the Air*, 4–5.

6 Clough, *The User Unconscious*, xii.

7 Manning, *The Minor Gesture*, 58.

8 Ruyer, *La genèse des forms vivantes*; quoted in Manning, *The Minor Gesture*, 58.

9 The *neuro* prefix in these terms is potentially misleading, as Manning is acutely aware that brains are productions of bodily ecological practices.

10 As will become clear, the parenthetical *in* is not an expression of authorial modesty, but an assertion that there is something incoherent about coherence. Indeed, I'm grateful to Josh Dittrich for pointing out that (in)coherence may itself be a key concept of this book's argument even in not being named as such, because it formulates the contradictory notions of inherence, excessiveness, coalescence, and particularity that characterize incommunication. More simply, this book proceeds from an assumption that the universe is not coherent with itself (i.e., there is no such thing as "the world," but rather worldings upon worldings that are always more-thans).

11 Serres, *The Parasite*, 13.

12 Manning, "Fugitively, Approximately," 10.

13 Serres, *The Parasite*, 63 and passim. Marie Thompson parses Serres's position specifically in the context of a sound studies argument about noise in chapter 2 of *Beyond Unwanted Sound*.

14 Galloway, Thacker, and Wark, *Excommunication*, 10.

15 Galloway, Thacker, and Wark, *Excommunication*, 15–16.

16 Thompson, *Beyond Unwanted Sound*, 62.

17 This position has certain elements of experience and perception a bit backward, as will become evident throughout this book.

18 Peters, *The Marvelous Clouds*, 44.

19 Eve Tuck and K. Wayne Yang make the consequences of one vector of such insidious scripting palpable in their agenda-setting article "Decolonization Is Not a Metaphor."

20 Galloway, "Peak Analog."

21 This perspective yields the corollary belief that the universe would be revealed to be fully determinate if we only had enough information. We don't need quantum physics to tell us that this isn't the case, although it does do just that.

22 Since this knowledge (and really, all knowledge) only appears as such in being communicated, communication always fails to succeed because the knowledge it shares discloses a not-knowing (in the form of a drive to know). See Connor, "Exopistemology."

23 Clough, *The User Unconscious*, xviii. Clough cites Latour, "'The Whole Is Always Smaller Than Its Parts,'" 595.

24 Krippendorf, cited in Umpleby, "Reviving the American Society for Cybernetics," 19.

25 There is, moreover, an urban legend—which may well be true—that companies use high match rankings as a future anterior psychological tactic. That is, an invented/inflated high match percentage increases individuals' confidence in a match, thus making it more likely that they will give the prospective relationship the benefit of the doubt, in turn making it more likely that the prediction will turn out to have been correct all along. There is thus a priming effect of the statistic that works despite nobody, at any point in the process, really understanding or believing the percentage (which belief would be impossible, given that the concept of a percentage in this context is literally meaningless).

26 Scannell, *Cities*.

27 To be clear, the process is validated even when folks (rightly) protest its perversion, as in the U.S. examples of "hanging chads" during the 2000 election or of Republicans frequently being elected with less than 50 percent of the popular vote. In both cases, the stakes of the argument are as high as they are because the (post)political reality is such that predicates of the electoral process itself are largely beyond the pale.

28 I, of course, am far from the first to use the term *afterlife* to mark the effective persistence of something beyond its seeming end. I first encountered this use of the term in graduate school during a seminar leading up to a public lecture to be given by Eugene Thacker (related, I believe, to his at that time unpublished book *After Life*). Today, this use of the term is probably most strongly associated with Saidiya Hartman, who uses the phrase "afterlife of slavery" to theorize how the subjection of Black people persists after the legal end of enslavement, and how this persistence is a continuance of the racial logics of slavery. See Hartman, *Lose Your Mother*.

29 Hong, "Technologies of Speculation."

30 This works in tandem with an opposite strategy that Ruha Benjamin calls the "datafication of injustice," where a claim of needing more data serves as a justification for inaction. That is, "the hunt for more and more data is a barrier for acting on what we already know." See Benjamin, *Race after Technology*, 78.

31 Obviously, the financial investment of technology corporations throughout the public sector plays a decisive role in this paradigm.

32 Fazi, "Can a Machine Think," 817–18, emphasis in original.

33 Fazi, "Can a Machine Think," 818.

34 Fazi, "Can a Machine Think," 818.

35 Fazi, "Can a Machine Think," 818.

36 Fazi, "Can a Machine Think," 818. It is important to note that Fazi presents this line of thinking in the context of her argument that computers might nonetheless be capable of novel behavior if they are thought outside of what she calls the "simulative paradigm" that is inherited from Turing's famous test. (She coins the phrase specifically to explain the post-Turing inheritance of a certain understanding of intelligence, be it human or machine.) Such novelty, for Fazi, could thereby "come not from breaking mechanical rules, but from following them," which is to say from doing "what computers do already."

37 Fazi, "Can a Machine Think," 819.

38 For Fazi, this invariance is best explained through an analysis of the simulative paradigm.

39 Galloway, "Peak Analog."

40 This is built into the word *data* itself, which names both a single monolithic conceptual entity and a swarm of particulars.

41 I'm drawing on the etymology and early use of the term *aphasia* here, using it adjectivally to convey the loss of communicative capacity that many people—including me—have experienced in stressful, frightening, or otherwise intensified situations (most frequently, as is germane to this book, in dreams). The (admittedly more common) use of the term to indicate a pathology resulting from damage to the brain bears a different kind of consideration, led by someone who lives with that pathology. (Nonetheless, my use of the term is in solidarity with a central tenet of much critical disability literature, namely, that *disability* names a particular situation—most often a societal exclusion—rather than an impairment per se. See Mankoff, Hayes, and Kasnitz, "Disability Studies as a Source of Critical Inquiry," 3. See also Joshua St. Pierre and Charis St. Pierre on the "disciplining of the tongue" involved in speech-language pathology in "Governing the Voice.")

42 Dean, "Communicative Capitalism," 59; cited in Behar, "Speaking Volumes."

43 Harney and Moten, *The Undercommons*, 19.

44 James, *The Sonic Episteme*, 8.

45 James, *The Sonic Episteme*, 5. James notes that Jonathan Sterne's oft-cited "audio-visual litany" charts similar terrain. See Sterne, *The Audible Past*, 15.

Notes to Introduction 137

46 James, *The Sonic Episteme*, 5.

47 James, *The Sonic Episteme*, 3.

48 James, *The Sonic Episteme*, 4.

49 James, *The Sonic Episteme*, 5–6.

50 I am grateful to the anonymous reader whose report I drew upon to formulate this paragraph.

Chapter One: Networking Sound and Medium Specificity

An earlier version of chapter 1 was published in *Evental Aesthetics* 2, no. 2 (2013) as "The Sonic Effect: Aurality and Digital Networks in Exurbia." Thank you to Mandy-Suzanne Wong and Joanna Demers for their editorial work in that setting.

1 This example borrows its impulse, if not its actual text or examples, from Wallace, *Everything and More*, 31. In the cited section, Wallace exemplifies the way that mathematics texts can tend to be "abstruse and technical . . . because of all the specifications and conditions that have to be put on theorems to keep them out of crevasses" (31n19). The question of finitude that this equation touches on in this chapter is taken up more fully in chapter 3.

2 This is the implicit drive of our initial diffidence toward the equation $\frac{x}{2} = \frac{x}{200}$, namely, that we know that if both sides of the equation are equal, and if both sides feature the same numerator, then the denominators should be the same.

3 Krauss, "Sculpture in the Expanded Field"; Youngblood, *Expanded Cinema*.

4 See Bal, *Traveling Concepts in the Humanities*, chapter 4. Bal notes that in contrast to the term *context*, the act of framing "produces an event [that is] performed by an agent who is responsible [for their] acts" and who is in turn framed by the action of framing in a potentially infinite regress that foregrounds the involvement of time (135–36).

5 See Derrida, *Of Grammatology*. Gayatri Spivak briefly discusses différance on pp. xx–lxxi in her "Translator's Introduction." Indeed, Spivak's introduction is notably lucid in parsing the vexing paradoxes that Derrida puts to work.

6 Pater, *The Renaissance*, 140.

7 Kim-Cohen, *In the Blink of an Ear*, 39. One might argue that paratextuality marks a similar vector in literary interpretation, but Kim-Cohen's general point stands.

8 There is increasingly work that takes up the position that music cannot be considered to be distinct from the physical-psychic experience of making and listening to music. For example, Nina Eidsheim's "Sensing Voice" treats music as an experience of the total sensorium and is particularly fascinating in this respect. I agree wholeheartedly, but would also point out that it is telling that even as recently as 2011 (and in a journal—*The Senses and Society*—that is not particular to musicology, no less!), Eidsheim feels compelled to begin her argument by distinguishing her methods from "common methods of musical representation and

analysis [because these tend to] evidence Western culture's preoccupation with what notation can capture and preserve" (134).

9 I use the term *rhetoric* in the broadest sense, to indicate methods of persuasion. Thus, for example, music is a method that persuades us that sounds can be selected and ordered such that they become meaningful, and specifically musically meaningful. In this approach to the term, I am grateful to Marcel O'Gorman.

10 Kim-Cohen, *In the Blink of an Ear*, 59.

11 To be clear, this is not a critique of music per se, nor is it a situation that is unique to music, but is rather a statement about how systems operate.

12 That is, if music is apolitical in this way, then it is also colonial, white supremacist, and sexist.

13 Kim-Cohen, *In the Blink of an Ear*, 107.

14 John Cage, quoted in Kostelanetz and Darby, *Classic Essays on Twentieth-Century Music*, 185.

15 Priest, *Boring Formless Nonsense*, 58–59.

16 Kahn, *Noise, Water, Meat*, 162. For a longer engagement with the whiteness at stake in Cage's "modest" listening, see Thompson, "Whiteness and the Ontological Turn in Sound Studies"; Piekut, "Sound's Modest Witness"; and Lewis, "Improvised Music after 1950."

17 Kahn, *Noise, Water, Meat*, 164.

18 Or, more accurately, turns toward conceptualism, as I am not referring to conceptual art specifically. In the context being presented here, Marcel Duchamp's urinal and Faith Ringgold's paintings are as conceptual as Robert Morris's boxes or Jackson Pollock's action paintings. In each case, the rhetoric of the work is explicitly taken up in discursive logics that exceed the work proper. Considered from this perspective, then, we can separate the movement of conceptualism that gains prominence and then fades (as does cubism, for example) from the legacies of making the role of discourse explicit that remain an active component of visual arts practice today.

19 Kim-Cohen, *In the Blink of an Ear*, 107.

20 Of course, "popular music" vexes this conventional, institutional understanding of music in entirely different ways, and a number of scholars (musicologists and otherwise) have convincingly shown that maintaining a boundary between concert music and popular music in the first place is conceptually unsustainable—and without that border, the entire discourse of pure music quickly falls apart. My argument here is meant to supplement that position, with which I wholly agree.

21 Kahn, *Noise, Water, Meat*, 190.

22 Chapter 5 significantly complicates this tendency to differentiate hearing and listening along the lines of concentration.

23 Importantly—and as is discussed elsewhere in this book—computers are in this sense grammatical machines.

24 Padui, "Realism, Anti-realism, and Materialism," 91–92; quoted in Wolfe, *Ecological Poetics*, 192n55.

25 Wolfe, *Ecological Poetics*, 83.

26 Kim-Cohen, *In the Blink of an Ear*, 259.

27 Kim-Cohen, *In the Blink of an Ear*, 99.

28 Kim-Cohen, *In the Blink of an Ear*, 97–98.

29 Kim-Cohen, *In the Blink of an Ear*, 98. See also Kittler, *Gramophone, Film, Typewriter*.

30 Kim-Cohen, *In the Blink of an Ear*, 100.

31 Kim-Cohen, *In the Blink of an Ear*, 100.

32 Kim-Cohen, *In the Blink of an Ear*, 233. As an example, offered by Kim-Cohen, the text on the left side of the billboard begins with, "What do you see here? The text/sign to the right presents itself as something else, something we could normally take for granted," while that opposite it on the right reads, "Can you read this? This text/sign to the left expects you to read more than it provides, but it provides more than is needed to mean what it does."

33 Kim-Cohen, *In the Blink of an Ear*, 234.

34 Kim-Cohen, *In the Blink of an Ear*, 234.

35 Indeed, such a prioritization is even present in this sentence, which frames the text as the content of the two media.

36 Kim-Cohen, *In the Blink of an Ear*, 235.

37 For an excellent introduction to the relationship between second-order systems theory (SOST) and deconstruction, see Wolfe, "Meaning as Event-Machine." Niklas Luhmann situates SOST—which builds on Derrida's damning critique of systems theory in "Structure, Sign, and Play" and elsewhere—as "the reconstruction of deconstruction." See Luhmann, "How Can the Mind Communicate?" See also Derrida, "Structure, Sign, and Play in the Discourse of the Human Sciences."

38 Sterne, "Hearing, Listening, and Deafness," 20.

39 Quote from Dyson, *Sounding New Media*, 4.

40 LaBelle, *Background Noise*, xxv.

41 Girard, *Proofs and Types*, 2.

42 These modifications are all standard digital audio manipulations, including changes in amplitude, sample reversal, granulation, reverberation, and so on.

43 This is effectively impossible to do with complete accuracy.

44 For example, one could do an edit play-through of the volume parameter without making any alterations.

45 Of course, other approaches to electronic music can also be cumbersome, and microsound and tape composers often see their work as physical, messy interactions with actual material, even though their work is digital. See, for example, the chapter "Minimal Objects in Microsound" in Demers, *Listening through the Noise*. However, I would argue that the frustration of working with *Exurbia* I am

discussing here is distinct from such cases and is in some senses the opposite: unless one tunes into the strange mode of listening that *Exurbia* suggests, it is difficult to feel as though one is making a mess because one's actions (insofar as they even are one's) are diffused through an interface that makes them slow, coarse, invisible, and of limited efficacy. The frustration of composing with *Exurbia* is more akin to that of trying to fix a computer by rebooting it than it is to the trope of playing in a digital sandbox.

46 There is an apt resonance in this respect between *Exurbia* and early electronic instruments developed prior to screen-based user interfaces. A key difference remains the network component of the piece, though, which acts like an (unprecedentedly large) intercomputer patching system.

47 Taken together, *Exurbia* both temporalizes sound and makes it plastic, in Catherine Malabou's sense of (paradoxically) retaining traces of older forms while and by morphing into new ones. See Malabou, *What Should We Do with Our Brain?*

48 Certain observations about sound's medium specificity in the section below are borrowed from the introduction to my book *Humanesis*. Specifically, I argue there that sound can be characterized as a simultaneous palpation of four medial vectors: it is semiotically parasitic, differentially and temporally embodied, relational, and multiplicitous.

49 Evens, *Sound Ideas*, 1.

50 Evens, *Sound Ideas*, 1.

51 Tinnitus offers a special, fascinating, and not yet entirely understood exception to this scenario that, in Steven Connor's hands, redoubles the paradox I'm alluding to. See Connor, "Ausculations." More recently, Mack Hagood has thoroughly unpacked the vexatious and elusive character of tinnitus in the (brilliant) first chapter of *Hush*.

52 Prelistening edits would routinely include cutting excess material at the beginning and end of clips, volume normalization, noise cancellation, and so on.

53 Moreover, this slowness isn't just a matter of the pieces taking more time to make and to listen to, but also manifests in the sounds of the works produced: the decreased editing acuity that is a paradoxical companion to this slowness results in a kind of coarseness or clunkiness that is particular to the environment. Where compositions produced with Pro Tools might dance lithely across the stereo field, *Exurbia*'s compositions tend to stumble along with the impotently brute movements of a toddling child.

54 This is of course not always the case as there is significant variance both within and between individuals. However, there is some evidence that music seems to more regularly induce involuntary semantic memories. Victoria Williamson conjectures that this may be because "music is more deeply encoded than words. Music activates multiple brain areas (usually more than simply hearing words) and can activate some of the deepest reward centres. And if something has more connections in the mind then it is more likely that it will be re-activated

compared to something with fewer connections." See Williamson, "Earworm Interview."

55 Behar, *Bigger Than You*, internal quote from page 3.

56 Madrigal, "Dark Social."

57 This collective element, too, is captured in Behar's "decelerationism" coinage.

58 *Griefing* is a term typically used in the context of online gaming to indicate a harmful action done to another player through the means provided by the game's design. In the case of *Exurbia*, one composer overwrote a large number of samples with silence (see Urban Dictionary, "Griefer").

59 There is a rich history of this approach in the arts, as well as other fields. Notably, Manning and Massumi propose emphasizing process over "deliverable products" as an element of constructing "the conditions for a speculative pragmatism" (*Thought in the Act*, 89–91).

60 Brenda Laurel, cited in Dyson, *Sounding New Media*, 140.

Chapter Two: Listening and Technicity

I previously discussed the Fathead project that anchors this chapter in *symploke* 23, nos. 1–2 (2015), though in very different ways and to very different ends. Thanks to Nathan Snaza for the invitation to do so, and for his tweaks to that offering. A few paragraphs from this chapter were published as "An( )Alibic Aural Tetrad: A Fourfold Structure of Ecologicity" in *Plastic Blue Marble* (Victoria: Noxious Sector Press, 2016). I appreciate Ted Hiebert's editorial work in that setting, as well as the insightful and encouraging critical attention that Amanda Boetzkes gave that writing.

1 There are myriad possible variations of this setup, with the simplest (and in some ways most remarkable) being one that simply reverses the auditor's stereo field by placing the left microphone on the right ear (and vice versa).

2 As I'll discuss more generally, my listening through my feet in this way is qualitatively different than the pedic listening undertaken by elephants, robins, and certain other animals, reptiles, and insects.

3 This aligns with Seth Kim-Cohen's emphasis on the noncochlear in listening, as well as Douglas Kahn's insistence on the discursive element in listening that motivates his critique of Cage, both discussed in chapter 1.

4 Lastra, "Fidelity vs. Intelligibility," 251.

5 James, *Sonic Episteme*.

6 William Brent helped me extensively with the technical elements of several Fathead experiments. Adam Tindale also offered technical assistance in the initial stages of experimentation and was particularly helpful in making certain technical constraints clear to me.

7 As Wikipedia, "Inverse-Square Law," summarizes: "The inverse-square law,

in physics, is any physical law stating that a specified physical quantity or intensity is inversely proportional to the square of the distance from the source of that physical quantity." It is worth noting that while simple temporal delay and volume diminution play a large role in spatializing sound, there are plenty of other factors as well. Moreover, ears are by no means the only locus of hearing. "Inverse-Square Law," Wikipedia, accessed December 10, 2019, https://en.wikipedia.org/wiki/Inverse-square_law.

8 Despite living in a (mostly) metric country (and generally thinking in metric measurements), I was seduced by the round number into using the imperial measure.

9 Wikipedia, "Raspberry Pi": "The Raspberry Pi is a series of small single-board computers developed in the United Kingdom by the Raspberry Pi Foundation to promote teaching of basic computer science in schools and in developing countries. The original model became far more popular than anticipated, selling outside its target market for uses such as robotics. It does not include peripherals (such as keyboards and mice) or cases. However, some accessories have been included in several official and unofficial bundles." "Raspberry Pi," Wikipedia, accessed December 19, 2019, https://en.wikipedia.org/wiki/Raspberry_Pi.

10 There is an important technical constraint that bears consideration, detailed discussion of which I have postponed to chapter 3.

11 A three-minute sample is available on my website at http://www.davidcecchetto.net/downloads/fathead_lad.mp3.

12 A half second is approximate, because it depends on how far in front of one the source of the sound is.

13 Hansen, "Shi Jian."

14 Hansen, *Bodies in Code*, 9.

15 See the analogous discussion of psychology in the introduction.

16 I've indeed remarked on these experiences in Cecchetto, "Four Experiments in Broadband Auralneirics."

17 It follows from this that the accuracy of depth perception changes dramatically based on the direction.

18 See the work of Humberto R. Maturana and his various collaborators cited in Hayles, *How We Became Posthuman*, 131–59; Uexküll, *A Foray into the Worlds of Animals and Humans*; and Bateson, *Steps to an Ecology of Mind*.

19 "Regime of Computation" from Hayles, *My Mother Was a Computer*.

20 In chapter 3 I consider M. Beatrice Fazi's analysis of the simulative paradigm in computing to show how every computational communication fails for analogous reasons. Shane Denson describes this sort of scalar infolding through the concept of "discorrelation" that he develops brilliantly throughout *Discorrelated Images*.

21 Hayles, "Traumas of Code," 137–38.

22 A joke to illustrate the perspectivalism of what is realistic: "A Canadian

soldier was friends with Pablo Picasso, but their friendship included the soldier openly admitting to Picasso that he did not like the abstraction of his art because it was not realistic. One day, the soldier returns to Europe after having been on leave in Canada for several months, and tells his friend that he has married someone during that time. Picasso is happy for his friend and asks to see a picture of the new bride, which the soldier produces in the form of a locket. Taking the locket, Picasso cannot hide his distaste for the photo, and—after several moments—says with disbelief: 'Does she really look like this?!' The soldier is obviously offended, and responds by extolling the beauties of his new wife, defending his love of her hair, complexion, profile, and figure. Picasso interrupts him impatiently, though, and exclaims, 'That is all well and good, but the woman I am looking at is no more than two inches tall!'"

23 Hansen, *Feed-Forward*, 36.

24 See Cecchetto, "An( )Alibic Aural Tetrad."

25 Munster, *Materializing New Media*, 50.

26 For any instructors who may be interested, I've included a short Aural Incommunications Seminar Prompt (with instructions) as an appendix to this book, which includes some instructions for making prosthetic devices. I have led (and would be delighted to lead again) such a seminar by invitation, but the prompt is designed to be modifiable so that I needn't be involved.

27 Limited documentation of some of the Tuning Speculation conferences—to date seven, plus satellite events—is available at The Occulture (http://www .theocculture.net).

28 Munster, "Tuning in to the Signaletic," emphasis added.

Chapter Three: Incomputable and Integral Incommunications

1 Hansen, *Feed-Forward*, 4.

2 Quote from Klaus Krippendorff, cited in Umpleby, "Reviving the American Society for Cybernetics," 19. This quotation has also been attributed to Heinz Von Foerster.

3 While code seems to offer a human-readable site of potential intervention, it is worth recalling Katherine Hayles's observation (which I cite in chapter 2) that "since large programs—say, Microsoft Word—are written by many programmers and portions of the code are recycled from one version to the next, no living person understands the programs in their totality." Hayles, "Traumas of Code," 137–38.

4 Hansen, *Feed-Forward*, 134.

5 Discussed at length in chapter 2, Fathead began as a wearable interface that alters the scale of the wearer's auditory *Umwelt*; in effect, various versions of the prototype differently simulate how it would sound to have a one-thousand-foot-wide head. The most basic prototypes consist of binaural microphones mounted to noise-canceling earphones, with the microphone signals routed through a processor in order to create the simulation.

6 It would theoretically be possible to use software to distinguish between various sound sources and separate these out for calculation, but doing so with currently available wearable computing hardware would introduce a processing lag that would itself puncture the integrity of the simulation.

7 This is not to say that one can't learn something from wearing it in quotidian contexts, but only that the effect in that case would not be simulative.

8 See Anthony Enns's translator's introduction to Ernst, *Chronopoetics*, xx.

9 Ernst, *Sonic Time Machines*, 68, emphasis added.

10 Sprenger, *The Politics of Micro-decisions*, 97.

11 Sprenger, *The Politics of Micro-decisions*, 98.

12 Sprenger, *The Politics of Micro-decisions*, 98.

13 Sprenger, *The Politics of Micro-decisions*, 98.

14 If I say, for example, that the coronavirus pandemic, the Trump reelection campaign, and the murder of George Floyd happened simultaneously in 2020, I'm not saying they took place at the exact same moment but am instead indicating a certain temporality of political operations.

15 See, for example, Fazi, "Can a Machine Think?," which I mention in the introduction of this book, where Fazi works to reframe computer intelligence in terms other than Turing's simulative paradigm. She furthers this reframing in "Beyond Human."

16 Fazi, "Incomputable Aesthetics."

17 Fazi, "Incomputable Aesthetics"; Parisi, quoted in Clough, *The User Unconscious*, xv.

18 Fazi, *Contingent Computation*, 114; Dutilh Novaes, *Formal Languages in Logic*, 17.

19 Or, more precisely, the idea that there are facts which are in principle unknowable is a senseless one. This aspect of pragmatism is briefly discussed in the introduction to this book.

20 See Hayles, "Virtual Bodies and Flickering Signifiers," as well as its slightly revised reprinting as chapter 2 in *How We Became Posthuman*.

21 Goldblatt, *Topoi*, 174.

22 Goldblatt, *Topoi*, 175.

23 Goldblatt, *Topoi*, 174.

24 Goldblatt, *Topoi*, 176.

25 Goldblatt, *Topoi*, 176. This was particularly significant with respect to conceptualizations of infinitude, as Brouwer rejected the "conception of infinite collections as things-in-themselves" (Goldblatt, *Topoi*, 176). This bears directly on the question of computability, as I discuss below.

26 Bateson famously said of George Creel, "He was an applied scientist before the science was ripe to be applied." Bateson, *Steps to an Ecology of Mind*, 480.

27 Brouwer, *Collected Works*, vol. 1, 480. See again the "pragmatic maxim" discussed in the introduction.

28 Brouwer, *Collected Works*, vol. 1, 480.

29 Goldblatt, *Topoi*, 176.

30 Goldblatt, *Topoi*, 176. Of course, the understanding of language from which Brouwer distinguishes mathematics is not one by which many contemporary, post-Derridean thinkers would abide.

31 Goldblatt, *Topoi*, 177.

32 Goldblatt, *Topoi*, 177.

33 For his part, it was important to Gödel to explicitly state that his theorem VI (the so-called first incompleteness theorem) was constructive, and specifically "proved in an intuitionistically unobjectionable manner." For a more extended discussion of this influence, see "Brouwer-Hilbert Controversy," Wikipedia, accessed April 21, 2021, https://en.wikipedia.org/wiki/Brouwer%E2%80%93Hilbert_controversy.

34 Fazi, "Incomputable Aesthetics."

35 Fazi, "Incomputable Aesthetics." This indicates an aesthetic grounding because, as Steven Shaviro notes in a different context, "it is only aesthetically, beyond understanding and will, that I can appreciate the actus of the thing being what it is." Cited in Clough, *The User Unconscious*, xvi.

36 Fazi, "Incomputable Aesthetics."

37 Fazi, "Incomputable Aesthetics."

38 Fazi, "Incomputable Aesthetics."

39 Fazi, "Incomputable Aesthetics."

40 Hansen, "After Machines," 74.

41 Hansen, "After Machines," 76.

42 Hansen, "After Machines," 78.

43 Hansen, "After Machines," 79.

44 Hansen, "After Machines," 88.

45 Hansen, "After Machines," 87.

46 Ernst, cited in Hansen, "After Machines," 79.

47 This relates to Landauer's Principle, which states that the entropy decrease of the "information bearing" degrees of freedom during a logically irreversible operation must be compensated by an equal or greater entropy increase in the non-information-bearing degrees of freedom and environment. See Bennett, "Notes on Landauer's Principle, Reversible Computation and Maxwell's Demon," for a more robust discussion of the principle, its implications, and objections to it.

48 Hansen, *Feed-Forward*, 80. See my discussion of this (in tandem with The Occulture) in chapter 1 of Cecchetto et al., *Ludic Dreaming*, particularly pages 27–29.

49 Galloway, "Peak Analog."

50 An explanation of the harmonic series would be an unnecessary detour here. Suffice it to say that overtones are what make the same pitch sound different when it is played on different instruments (for example, on a violin rather than on

a trumpet). The fundamental pitch may be the same—and the overtone series is the same for any instance of a given fundamental pitch—but the tone is colored by the relative intensity of each overtone, which intensities differ from instrument to instrument (and between different registers on the same instrument such that, for example, a high note on a classical guitar might sound brittle while a low note may seem booming).

51 Galloway, "Peak Analog." Galloway points out that "a corollary to this is that frequency/harmonics as such are digital technologies, or at least proto-digital."

52 We might say, then, that there is a time-criticality of violin sounds: what we hear as a single or simultaneous tone is actually a linear sequence of acoustic/ vibratory/material moments. Acoustic timbre (sequenced not just as a simultaneity of overtones, but also as a sequence of attack, variable sustain, decay, and release) has its own specific temporal dimension.

53 Hansen, "Symbolizing Time," 225.

54 Hansen, "Symbolizing Time," 229. Irreversibility enters this discussion because it pertains to the ongoingness of temporalization. That is, since a given process and its temporal production are immanent to one another, to reverse the process would be to produce a reversed temporalization rather than to reverse time itself (i.e., since there is no such thing as time itself).

55 See, as only a few more recent examples of many, Chude-Sokei, *The Sound of Culture*; Crawley, *Blackpentecostal Breath*; Hagood, *Hush*; Robinson, *Hungry Listening*; Stoever, *The Sonic Color Line*; and Thompson, *Beyond Unwanted Sound*. More canonical examples can be found throughout the work of Jonathan Sterne, as well as in musicological discourses since the 1990s.

56 The process is different because it is internal to the computer, but Alvin Lucier's canonical *I Am Sitting in a Room* (1969) offers a good point of reference for the resulting sound.

57 Wikipedia tends to cover the technical elements of these well; see "Window Function," Wikipedia, accessed April 21, 2012, https://en.wikipedia.org/wiki /Window_function.

58 It's worth noting in this context that windowing is used in ultrasound scanning, and is a perfect example of the kind of unacknowledged skilled work performed by technicians (who are paid less than doctors, and who are disproportionately women and often women of color) who delicately tune the machines to each person's different body to get at what they want to see. That is, windowing might seem to be an objective technical operation, because acknowledging its artfulness would upset the medical hierarchy by making the skill of this labor visible.

59 Relatedly, Hugh S. Manon and Daniel Temkin point out that *glitch* "does not solely represent the cause that initiates some failure, but also the output that results when improper data is decoded properly." Manon and Temkin, "Notes on Glitch." Since computation proceeds from incomputability—that is, a primary de-

termination of (im)propriety—all computation is in some sense glitchy. (I'm grateful to Shane Denson for this reference.)

60 Goldin and Wegner, "The Interactive Nature of Computing," 18.

61 As with *scale*, the term *sound* is also materially-semiotically constituted according to these particularities of its computation. See, for example, the interrogation of the concept of *the sound itself* threaded throughout chapter 1.

62 Again, these features have been convincingly critiqued by sound studies, most notably through Jonathan Sterne's discussion of the "audiovisual litany" in *The Audible Past*, 15. My point here is that they become untenable in different ways when considered in light of their computation.

63 As Serres outlines, "either there *is* a private dimension, in which case there are not objective messages; or the latter are in fact in circulation, in which case there is no private dimension." Serres, *The Five Senses*, 139. I further explore the otoacoustic dimension of listening—as well as its incommunicative import—in chapter 5.

64 Hagood, *Hush*, 61. As Hagood accounts, "due to the painstaking pitch and volume matching, these two sounds now blend together at the limens of internal and external, body and mind, real and imaginary, subject and object. 'I think that's it,' says [the person experiencing tinnitus]. '*Now I'm not sure what's me and what's you [i.e., the person controlling the audiometric tone].*'" Hagood, *Hush*, 61.

65 Fazi, "Incomputable Aesthetics."

Chapter Four: Algorithms, Art, and Sonicity

Chapter 4 includes significant material that was published (in an earlier form) in *The Routledge Companion to Sounding Art* (New York: Routledge, 2017), though the argument has been updated and readings added. I'm grateful to Barry Truax and the other editors of that collection for their work on the original chapter.

1 James, *Sonic Intimacy*, 6.

2 Originally, DNA was "seen" with an electron microscope, which produces a negative image based on the reflection of electrons rather than light.

3 LaBelle, *Background Noise*, 62.

4 Nancy, *Listening*. The particular phrase "resounds beyond significance" is not from Nancy's text, but from Lars Iyer's blurb.

5 *Ransom Notes* can be viewed on Vimeo (https://vimeo.com/53006805).

6 To ask the question in that way is part of—or perhaps a perversion of—what Heidegger means with the concept of something being "ready-to-hand," which he describes as a special kind of sight that guides our manipulation of a thing at a level that we can never get at just by looking at it or thinking about it. Importantly for the present consideration, this readiness-to-hand is exactly what is specific about the thing in question; it is what differentiates *Ransom Notes* from another film that might have all of the same components of text, sound, and so on.

7   This is not to wax romantic about art: the antischematic undercurrent of this book (and the incommunication gambit it makes) is similarly amethodological. Likewise, there is a strong antimethodological vector ranging across contemporary theory, ranging from Derrida's declaration that grammatology is not a methodology, to Ashon Crawley's claim that writing blackness requires a rejection of methods, to Judith Roof's queer, feminist readings of DNA's contingent poetics (to name only a few that spring to mind).

8   For the first part, the problem of "being able to make" is something of a false one, as this is simply a description of anything; all that exists is caught up in the ongoing unfolding of the worldly incoherences that constitute making.

9   Hansen, "New Media," 172.

10   Hansen, *Feed-Forward*, 6.

11   Merz, "Method for Simulating Creativity."

12   Merz has experimented with numerous cellular automata as well as swarm intelligence algorithms in his other works.

13   Schilling, "A 'Small-World' Network Model of Cognitive Insight," 130.

14   See Milgram, "The Small World Problem."

15   See Hayles, *My Mother Was a Computer*.

16   Ross, *The Rest Is Noise*, 370.

17   Connor, "Earslips," 7.

18   "Speculative aesthetics" from Drucker and Nowviskie, "Speculative Computing."

19   Munster, *An Aesthesia of Networks*, 35.

20   Walker and Nees, "Theory of Sonification," 9.

21   Kubisch, "Electrical Walks."

22   Kim-Cohen, *In the Blink of an Ear*, 115.

23   This is, of course, the case with all listening. The point I'm making isn't about aesthetic listening as opposed to quotidian listening but that aesthetic listening is a part of all listening that is made explicit in listening to aesthetic propositions—or rather, in listening to propositions in their aesthetic profile.

24   James, *The Writings of William James*, 269; cited in Munster, *An Aesthesia of Networks*, 41.

25   See Manning, *Always More Than One*.

26   Juliana Pivato, email message to author, April 16, 2014.

27   Pivato, email, April 16, 2014.

28   *Freezing* can be viewed on Colin Clark's website (https://colinclark.org/videos/freezing/).

29   Hansen, *Feed-Forward*, 54.

30   Colin Clark, email message to author, May 11, 2020.

31   Biennale di Venezia, *May You Live in Interesting Times*, 81. For a discussion of the data sublime, see Stallabrass, "What's in a Face?"

32   It isn't my intention here to evaluate this work one way or another: I cer-

Notes to Chapter Four   149

tainly agree that it is problematic—especially in the meaning and authenticity he ascribes to the rawness of data—but it is also more complex in the particular than a generic reading of the work can capture.

33 Biennale di Venezia, *May You Live in Interesting Times*, 75.

34 Given the hegemony of European and North American artists in the global art market, it is also worth noting that the piece makes a place for cultural knowledge that is not always validated in such settings.

35 More information about RTSW is available on Renée Lear's website (http://reneelear.com/renee-taking-a-sip-of-water-human-and-video-in-motion/).

36 See Lear's website.

37 Galloway, Thacker, and Wark, *Excommunication*, 40.

38 Munster, *An Aesthesia of Networks*, 3.

39 Munster, *An Aesthesia of Networks*, 32.

Chapter Five: Listening and Technicity (Once and for All, Again and Again)

A few paragraphs from chapter 5 were published as "An( )Alibic Aural Tetrad: A Four-fold Structure of Ecologicity," in *Plastic Blue Marble* (Victoria: Noxious Sector Press, 2016). I appreciate Ted Hiebert's editorial work in that setting, as well as the insightful and encouraging critical attention that Amanda Boetzkes gave that writing.

1 Together, these bones are called the auditory ossicles.

2 I discuss this briefly in chapter 4, and more extensively (but obliquely) in the first chapter.

3 This process is also nonreversible, and thus extremely "lossy" from an informational perspective.

4 Evens, *Sound Ideas*, 16.

5 Boetzkes, "Interpretation and the Affordance of Things," 288. I have substituted "determinable" and "indeterminable" for Boetzkes's use of "visible" and "invisible" in order to avoid certain confusions. While this substitution aligns—to my mind—with her argument in this case, this is not to suggest that it obtains more broadly. Clearly, Boetzkes's work—in the cited chapter and elsewhere—works through the operations of (in)visibility in concert with specific aesthetic regimes of visibility as well as specific ocular and neuroscientific discourses related to the eye, none of which nuance would be captured in the terminological substitution I've made here.

6 Hagood, *Hush*, 62.

7 For a discussion of "psychedelic adjacency," see Couroux, "Preemptive Glossary for a Techno-sonic Control Society."

8 Bateson, *Steps to an Ecology of Mind*, 144.

9 I discuss this in chapter 1 in the context of *Exurbia*.

10 Michel de Certeau, cited in Bassett, "Twittering Machines," 294.

11 Connor, "Earslips."

12 I discuss this via the psychological phenomenon known as "high-place phenomenon," developed by Jennifer Hames and her collaborators, in Cecchetto, "An( )Alibic Aural Tetrad." See Hames et al., "An Urge to Jump Affirms the Urge to Live"; a commentary for lay audiences on Hames's study is available in Alexander, "That Weird Urge to Jump Off a Bridge, Explained."

13 As I discussed with respect to art making in chapter 4—specifically in the context of a work by Kelly Egan—the temporalities in play are incompatible.

14 Peters, *Speaking into the Air*, 16.

15 The popular acronym for Graphics Interchange Format is GIF, which can be used for small animations and (relatively low-resolution) video clips.

16 With respect to listening with eyes, there is something to be said about "sign music" and its proliferation on YouTube—more than just signed interpretations of lyrics, this is a genre of music that is elaborated through physical, a-semantic, signing; something akin to (often stationary) dance, but with a very different syntax. Increasingly, this genre also makes use of postproduction video-editing techniques, such that—as with audio music—certain strains are part of a "recording native" performance practice.

17 The allusion here to W. J. T. Mitchell's well-known book *What Do Pictures Want?* is intentional, not least because that book understands pictures (and I understand video games) as "complex assemblages of virtual, material, and symbolic elements." See Mitchell, *What Do Pictures Want?*, xiii.

18 Insofar as this tendency to fetishize athleticism connects to the racialized commodification and quantification of players, one could hear Curry's creative elaborations as fugitive expressions of joyful (Black) freedoms.

Postscript: Epidemiological Afterlives

1 I'm aware that numerous epidemiologists have long predicted a global pandemic such as the current one. My point is that such predictions are necessarily general and thus do not—and, to be clear, do not claim to—predict this particular outbreak.

2 Chun, "Crisis, Crisis, Crisis," 160.

3 Chun, "Crisis, Crisis, Crisis," 139.

4 I discussed this collaboration, titled *Skewed Remote Musical Performance*, in chapter 6 of my book *Humanesis*. I discuss another collaboration with William Brent, *Exurbia*, in chapter 1 of this book, and William also implemented the technical elements of some of the more complex Fathead prototypes.

5 The interface for our collaboration, which is called OUTPUT, was created and designed by William, and implemented using the open-source Pure Data programming environment. While we've tweaked it collaboratively during our work together, the technical achievement is entirely William's.

6 William designed the OUTPUT interface and describes it (and bytebeat music) as follows: "OUTPUT uses so-called 'bytebeat' algorithms as the foundation of its sound. Bytebeat music is produced by computing simple (often very short) formulas and treating the output values as samples within a digital audio stream. At the most basic level, these formulas have only one input variable that represents time, and increases by 1 for every desired sample of output. As the input time variable moves forward, the output produced at each time step is determined by the algorithm being used. In classic bytebeat music, the audio streams produced by these algorithms were fed to a digital/analog converter using a sampling rate of 8000Hz and bit depth of 8 (hence the name bytebeat). The technique produces audio signals with a surprising level of rhythmic, melodic, and timbral variation given the simplicity at its core.

"To understand the basic technical process, consider the simplest possible algorithm, which consists of only the time variable t. At the first time step, $t = 0$, and it increments by 1 at each subsequent step. When using a resolution of 8 bits, values for t will be interpreted within a range of 0 and 255 (an 8-bit number has 256 possible states). Input values of t that go beyond this range result in an output value that wraps back around to the minimum of 0. Thus, given an input t that starts at 0 and forever increments by 1, the resulting output over time will be a rising ramp that resets back to its low point each time it hits the maximum value of 255. As long as the repetition of this ramp occurs at an audible rate (20Hz or higher), we can listen to the signal and recognize it as a sawtooth waveform. This behavior can be changed by adding a mathematical operator and a constant value. For instance, $t*2$ multiplies the time variable by 2, which means that the high point of the ramp will be reached twice as fast. In terms of the resulting signal, this has the effect of raising the frequency of the sawtooth wave by an octave. Adding several operators, constants, and other variables increases the complexity of the resulting sound dramatically and chaotically. [For example,] to understand the eventual musical function of the variables $p0, p1, \ldots, p9$ in this algorithm:

$$
\begin{aligned}
&(\\
&\qquad (t \gg p0) * (p1 \,\&\\
&\qquad\qquad\quad (2291706249 \gg\\
&\qquad\qquad\qquad\qquad (t \gg p2 \,\&\, 30)\\
&\qquad\qquad\qquad)\\
&\qquad\qquad)\\
&\& \,255) +\\
&(\\
&\qquad (\\
&\qquad\qquad (\\
&\qquad\qquad\qquad (t \gg p3 \,|\\
&\qquad\qquad\qquad\qquad (t \gg p4)
\end{aligned}
$$

152   Notes to Postscript

$$| \; t \gg 8)$$
$$^* p5 + 4 \; ^*$$
$$($$
$$($$
$$(t \gg p6)$$
$$\& \; t \gg p7)$$
$$| \; t \gg p8)$$
$$)$$
$$\& \; 255)$$
$$\gg p9)$$

requires experimentation and practice, as some sonic features of the result are determined by the interaction of multiple parameters.

"OUTPUT is a system for networked performers to improvise with these algorithms by freely changing bit depth, sampling rate, and parameter values. To enable relationships between individual algorithms and inject elements of human control, players can clone each other's settings, synchronize time variables, automate performed parameter changes, and control a range of standard audio environment elements." William Brent, email message to author, May 29, 2020.

7 "Simply stated, JACK is a recursive acronym for JACK Audio Connection Kit which is a sound server (and more!) that will serve audio to applications that request it. But merely calling JACK a 'sound server' belies its other powerful, pervasive aspects and capabilities. Indeed, JACK provides the audio backbone for Linux audio and all serious audio distributions not only include it, but have come to rely on it." Ubuntu Documentation, "What Is JACK," accessed April 27, 2021, https://help.ubuntu.com/community/What%20is%20JACK.

BIBLIOGRAPHY

Adorno, Theodor. *Lectures on Negative Dialectics*. Edited by Rolf Tiedemann. Translated by Rodney Livingstone. Cambridge: Polity, 2008.

Alexander, Brian. "That Weird Urge to Jump Off a Bridge, Explained." NBC News, March 13, 2012. https://nbcnews.com/healthmain/weird-urge-jump-bridge-explained-424037.

Bal, Mieke. *Travelling Concepts in the Humanities: A Rough Guide*. Toronto: University of Toronto Press, 2002.

Bassett, Caroline. "Twittering Machines: Antinoise and Other Tricks of the Ear." *differences: A Journal of Feminist Cultural Studies* 22, no. 2–3 (2011): 276–99.

Bateson, G. *Steps to an Ecology of Mind: Collected Essays in Anthropology, Psychiatry, Evolution, and Epistemology*. Chicago: University of Chicago Press, 1972.

Behar, Katherine. *Bigger Than You: Big Data and Obesity: An Inquiry towards Decelerationist Aesthetics*. New York: Punctum, 2016.

Behar, Katherine. "Speaking Volumes." Paper presented at Tuning Speculation IV, Toronto, November 18, 2016.

Benjamin, Ruha. *Race after Technology: Abolitionist Tools for the New Jim Code*. Cambridge: Polity, 2019.

Bennett, Charles H. "Notes on Landauer's Principle, Reversible Computation and Maxwell's Demon." *Studies in History and Philosophy of Modern Physics* 34 (2003): 501–10.

Biennale di Venezia. *May You Live in Interesting Times: Short Guide*. Edited by Flavia Fossa Margutti et al. Venice: Fondazione la Biennale di Venezia, 2019.

Boetzkes, Amanda. "Interpretation and the Affordance of Things." In *Heidegger and the Work of Art History*, edited by Amanda Boetzkes and Aron Vinegar, 269–91. Burlington, VT: Ashgate, 2014.

Brouwer, L. E. J. *Collected Works*. Vol. 1, *Philosophy and Foundations of Mathematics*. New York: American Elsevier, 1975.

Cecchetto, David. "An( )Alibic Aural Tetrad: A Fourfold Structure of Ecologicity." In *Plastic Blue Marble—Catalyst: Amanda Boetzkes*, edited by Ted Hiebert, 141–58. Victoria, Canada: Noxious Sector, 2016.

Cecchetto, David. "Four Experiments in Broadband Auralneirics." *symploke* 23, nos. 1–2 (2015): 111–18.

Cecchetto, David. *Humanesis: Sound and Technological Posthumanism*. Posthumanities 25. Minneapolis: University of Minnesota Press, 2013.

Cecchetto, David, with Marc Couroux, Ted Hiebert, and Eldritch Priest (as The Occulture). *Ludic Dreaming: How to Listen Away from Contemporary Technoculture*. London: Bloomsbury Academic, 2017.

Chude-Sokei, Louis. *The Sound of Culture: Diaspora and Black Technopoetics*. Middletown, CT: Wesleyan University Press, 2016.

Chun, Wendy. "Crisis, Crisis, Crisis: Or, The Temporality of Networks." In *The Nonhuman Turn*, edited by Richard Grusin, 139–66. Minneapolis: University of Minnesota Press, 2015.

Clough, Patricia Ticineto. *The User Unconscious: On Affect, Media, and Measure*. Minneapolis: University of Minnesota Press, 2018.

Connor, Steven. "Auscultations." Paper presented at Sonic Acts XIII, Amsterdam, February 27, 2010.

Connor, Steven. "Earslips: Of Mishearings and Mondegreens." Paper presented at Listening In, Feeding Back, Columbia University, February 14, 2009.

Connor, Steven. "Exopistemology: On Knowing without a Knower." Paper presented at Internationales Kolleg für Kulturtechnikforschung und Medienphilosophie, Weimar, May 23, 2018.

Couroux, Marc. "Preemptive Glossary for a Techno-sonic Control Society (with Lines of Flight) Pt. 3." *The Occulture* (blog), March 10, 2013. http://www.theocculture.net/preemptive3/.

Crawley, Ashon T. *Blackpentecostal Breath: The Aesthetics of Possibility*. New York: Fordham University Press, 2017.

Dean, Jodi. "Communicative Capitalism." *Cultural Politics* 1, no. 1 (2005): 51–74.

Demers, Joanna Teresa. *Listening through the Noise: The Aesthetics of Experimental Electronic Music*. Oxford: Oxford University Press, 2010.

Denson, Shane. *Discorrelated Images*. Durham, NC: Duke University Press, 2020.

Derrida, Jacques. *Of Grammatology*. Translated by Gayatri Spivak. Baltimore: Johns Hopkins University Press, 1976.

Derrida, Jacques. "Structure, Sign, and Play in the Discourse of the Human Sciences." In *Writing and Difference*, translated by Alan Bass, 278–93. Chicago: University of Chicago Press, 1978.

Drucker, Johanna, and Bethany Nowviskie. "Speculative Computing: Aesthetic Provocations in Humanities Computing." In *A Companion to Digital Humanities*, edited by Susan Schreibman, Ray Siemens, and John Unsworth. Oxford: Blackwell, 2004.

Dutilh Novaes, Catarina. *Formal Languages in Logic: A Philosophical and Cognitive Analysis*. Cambridge: Cambridge University Press, 2012.

Dyson, Frances. *Sounding New Media: Immersion and Embodiment in the Arts and Culture*. Berkeley: University of California Press, 2009.

Eidsheim, Nina Sun. "Sensing Voice: Materiality and the Lived Body in Singing and Listening." *Senses and Society* 6, no. 2 (2011): 133–55.

Ernst, Wolfgang. *Chronopoetics: The Temporal Being and Operativity of Technological Media*. Translated by Anthony Enns. London: Rowman and Littlefield, 2016.

Ernst, Wolfgang. *Sonic Time Machines: Explicit Sound, Sirenic Voices and Implicit Sonicity*. Amsterdam: Amsterdam University Press, 2016.

Evens, Aden. *Sound Ideas: Music, Machines, and Experience*. Theory Out of Bounds, 27. Minneapolis: University of Minnesota Press, 2005.

Fazi, M. Beatrice. "Beyond Human: Deep Learning, Explainability and Representation." *Theory, Culture and Society* (November 2020).

Fazi, M. Beatrice. "Can a Machine Think (Anything New)? Automation beyond Simulation." *AI and Society* 34 (2019): 813–24.

Fazi, M. Beatrice. *Contingent Computation: Abstraction, Experience and Indeterminacy in Computational Aesthetics*. London: Rowman and Littlefield, 2018.

Fazi, M. Beatrice. "Incomputable Aesthetics: Open Axioms of Contingency." *Computational Culture* 5 (2016). http://computationalculture.net/incomputable -aesthetics-open-axioms-of-contingency/.

Galloway, Alexander. "Peak Analog." *Culture and Communication* (blog), March 22, 2019. http://cultureandcommunication.org/galloway/peak-analog.

Galloway, Alexander R., Eugene Thacker, and McKenzie Wark. *Excommunication: Three Inquiries in Media and Mediation*. Chicago: University of Chicago Press, 2014.

Girard, Jean-Yves. *Proofs and Types*. Translated by Paul Taylor and Yves Lafont. Cambridge: Cambridge University Press, 1989.

Goldblatt, Robert. *Topoi: The Categorial Analysis of Logic*. Rev. ed. Mineola, NY: Dover, 2006.

Goldin, Dina, and Peter Wegner. "The Interactive Nature of Computing: Refuting the Strong Church-Turing Thesis." *Minds and Machines* 18 (2008): 17–38.

Hagood, Mack. *Hush: Media and Sonic Self-Control*. Durham, NC: Duke University Press, 2019.

Hames, Jennifer, Jessica D. Ribeiro, April R. Smith, and Thomas E. Joiner Jr. "An Urge to Jump Affirms the Urge to Live: An Empirical Examination of the High Place Phenomenon." *Journal of Affective Disorders* 136, no. 3 (2012): 1114–20.

Hansen, Mark B. N. "After Machines: Media Entangled Phenomenology." In *Philosophy after Nature*, edited by Rosi Braidotti and Rick Dolphijn, 73–98. New York: Rowman and Littlefield, 2017.

Hansen, Mark B. N. *Bodies in Code: Interfaces with Digital Media*. London: Routledge, 2006.

Hansen, Mark B. N. *Feed-Forward: On the Future of Twenty-First-Century Media*. Chicago: University of Chicago Press, 2015.

Hansen, Mark B. N. "New Media." In *Critical Terms for Media Studies*, edited by Mark B. N. Hansen and W. J. T. Mitchell, 172–85. Chicago: University of Chicago Press, 2010.

Hansen, Mark B. N. "Shi Jian: Time." *Vectors Journal* 3, no. 2 (2012). http://vectors.usc.edu/projects/index.php?project=91.

Hansen, Mark B. N. "Symbolizing Time: Kittler and Twenty-First-Century Media." In *Kittler Now: Current Perspectives in Kittler Studies*, edited by Stephen Sale and Laura Salisbury, 210–37. Cambridge: Polity, 2015.

Harney, Stefano, and Fred Moten. *The Undercommons: Fugitive Planning and Black Study*. Brooklyn, NY: Autonomedia, 2013.

Hartman, Saidiya. *Lose Your Mother: A Journey Along the Atlantic Slave Route*. New York: Farrar, Straus and Giroux, 2008.

Hayles, Katherine. *How We Became Posthuman: Virtual Bodies in Cybernetics, Literature and Informatics*. Chicago: University of Chicago Press, 1999.

Hayles, Katherine. *My Mother Was a Computer: Digital Subjects and Literary Texts*. Chicago: University of Chicago Press, 2005.

Hayles, Katherine. "Traumas of Code." *Critical Inquiry* 33, no. 1 (2006): 136–57.

Hayles, Katherine. "Virtual Bodies and Flickering Signifiers." *October* 66 (1993): 69–91.

Hong, Sun-Ha. "Technologies of Speculation." Public lecture at Infoscape Research Lab, Ryerson University (online), October 2, 2020.

James, Malcolm. *Sonic Intimacy: Reggae Sound Systems, Jungle Pirate Radio, and Grime YouTube Music Videos*. London: Bloomsbury, 2020.

James, Robin. *The Sonic Episteme: Acoustic Resonance, Neoliberalism, and Biopolitics*. Durham, NC: Duke University Press, 2019.

James, William. *The Writings of William James: A Comprehensive Edition*. Edited by John J. McDermott. Chicago: University of Chicago Press, 1978.

Kahn, Douglas. *Noise, Water, Meat: A History of Sound in the Arts*. Cambridge, MA: MIT Press, 1999.

Kim-Cohen, Seth. *In the Blink of an Ear: Towards a Non-cochlear Sonic Art*. New York: Continuum, 2009.

Kittler, Friedrich A. *Gramophone, Film, Typewriter*. Translated by Geoffrey Winthrop-Young and Michael Wutz. Stanford, CA: Stanford University Press, 1999.

Kostelanetz, Richard, and Joseph Darby, eds. *Classic Essays on Twentieth-Century Music: A Continuing Symposium*. New York: Schirmer, 1996.

Krauss, Rosalind E. "Sculpture in the Expanded Field." In *The Originality of the Avant-Garde and Other Modernist Myths*. Cambridge, MA: MIT Press, 1985.

Kubisch, Christina. "Electrical Walks." Accessed December 4, 2020. http://www.christinakubisch.de/en/works/electrical_walks.

LaBelle, Brandon. *Background Noise: Perspectives on Sound Art*. New York: Bloomsbury Academic, 2006.

Lastra, James. "Fidelity vs. Intelligibility." In *The Sound Studies Reader*, edited by Jonathan Sterne, 248–53. London: Routledge, 2012.

Latour, Bruno. "'The Whole Is Always Smaller Than Its Parts': A Digital Test of Gabriel Tardes' Monads." *British Journal of Sociology* 63, no. 4 (2012): 590–615.

Lewis, George. "Improvised Music after 1950: Afrological and Eurological Perspectives." *Black Music Research Journal* 16, no. 1 (1996): 91–122.

Luhmann, Niklas. "How Can the Mind Communicate?" In *Materialities of Communication*, edited by Hans Ulrich Gumbrecht and Karl Ludwig Pfeiffer, 371–88. Stanford, CA: Stanford University Press, 1994.

Madrigal, Alexis. "Dark Social: We Have the Whole History of the Web Wrong." *The Atlantic*, October 12, 2012. http://www.theatlantic.com/technology/archive/2012/10/dark-social-we-have-the-whole-history-of-the-web-wrong/263523/.

Malabou, Catherine. *What Should We Do with Our Brain?* Translated by Sebastian Rand. New York: Fordham University Press, 2008.

Mankoff, Jennifer, Gillian R. Hayes, and Devva Kasnitz. "Disability Studies as a Source of Critical Inquiry for the Field of Assistive Technology." In *Proceedings of the 12th International ACM SIGACCESS Conference on Computers and Accessibility: ASSETS '10*, 3. Orlando, FL: ACM Press, 2010.

Manning, Erin. *Always More Than One: Individuation's Dance*. Durham, NC: Duke University Press, 2013.

Manning, Erin. "Fugitively, Approximately." *Fibreculture Journal* 30 (2019): 10–23.

Manning, Erin. *The Minor Gesture*. Durham, NC: Duke University Press, 2016.

Manning, Erin, and Brian Massumi. *Thought in the Act: Passages in the Ecology of Experience*. Minneapolis: University of Minnesota Press, 2014.

Manon, Hugh S., and Daniel Temkin. "Notes on Glitch." *World Picture Journal* 6 (winter 2011). http://worldpicturejournal.com/WP_6/Manon.html.

Merz, Evan. "Method for Simulating Creativity to Generate Sound Collages from Documents on the Web." PhD diss., University of California–Santa Cruz, 2013.

Milgram, Stanley. "The Small World Problem." *Psychology Today* 2 (1967): 60–67.

Mitchell, W. J. T. *What Do Pictures Want? The Lives and Loves of Images*. Chicago: University of Chicago Press, 2005.

Munster, Anna. *An Aesthesia of Networks: Conjunctive Experience in Art and Technology*. Cambridge, MA: MIT Press, 2013.

Munster, Anna. *Materializing New Media: Embodiment in Information Aesthetics*. Dartmouth, NH: Dartmouth College Press, 2006.

Munster, Anna. "Tuning In to the Signaletic: Experiments with the Imperceptible of Real Time." Paper presented at Tuning Speculation III, Toronto, November 21, 2016.

Nancy, Jean-Luc. *Listening*. Translated by Charlotte Mandell. New York: Fordham University Press, 2007.

Padui, Raoni. "Realism, Anti-realism, and Materialism: Rereading the Critical Turn after Meilassoux." *Angelaki* 16, no. 2 (2011): 89–101.

Pater, Walter. *The Renaissance: Studies in Art and Poetry.* London: Macmillan, 1888.

Peters, John Durham. *The Marvelous Clouds: Toward a Philosophy of Elemental Media.* Chicago: University of Chicago Press, 2015.

Peters, John Durham. *Speaking into the Air: A History of the Idea of Communication.* Chicago: University of Chicago Press, 1999.

Piekut, Benjamin. "Sound's Modest Witness: Notes on Cage and Modernism." *Contemporary Music Review* 31, no. 1 (2012): 3–18.

Priest, Eldritch. *Boring Formless Nonsense: Experimental Music and the Aesthetics of Failure.* New York: Bloomsbury Academic, 2013.

Robinson, Dylan. *Hungry Listening: Resonant Theory for Indigenous Sound Studies.* Minneapolis: University of Minnesota Press, 2020.

Ross, Alex. *The Rest Is Noise: Listening to the Twentieth Century.* New York: Picador, 2008.

Ruyer, Raymond. *La genèse des formes vivantes.* Paris: Flammarion, 1958.

Scannell, Raymond Joshua. *Cities: Unauthored Resistances and Uncertain Sovereignty in the Urban World.* London: Routledge, 2016.

Schilling, Melissa A. "A 'Small-World' Network Model of Cognitive Insight." *Creativity Research Journal* 17, no. 2–3 (2005): 131–54.

Serres, Michel. *The Five Senses: A Philosophy of Mingled Bodies.* Translated by Margaret Sankey and Peter Cowley. London: Bloomsbury, 2008.

Serres, Michel. *The Parasite.* Translated by Lawrence R. Schehr. Minneapolis: University of Minnesota Press, 2007.

Sprenger, Florian. *The Politics of Micro-decisions: Edward Snowden, Net Neutrality, and the Architectures of the Internet.* Translated by Valentine A. Pakis. Lüneburg, Germany: Meson, 2015.

Stallabrass, Julian. "What's in a Face? Blankness and Significance in Contemporary Art Photography." *October* 122 (2007): 71–90.

Sterne, Jonathan. *The Audible Past: Cultural Origins of Sound Reproduction.* Durham, NC: Duke University Press, 2003.

Sterne, Jonathan. "Hearing, Listening, and Deafness." In *The Sound Studies Reader*, edited by Jonathan Sterne, 19–21. London: Routledge, 2012.

Stoever, Jennifer Lynn. *The Sonic Color Line: Race and the Cultural Politics of Listening.* New York: New York University Press, 2016.

St. Pierre, Joshua, and Charis St. Pierre. "Governing the Voice: A Critical History of Speech-Language Pathology." *Foucault Studies* 24 (2018): 151–84.

Thacker, Eugene. *After Life.* Chicago: University of Chicago Press, 2010.

Thompson, Marie. *Beyond Unwanted Sound: Noise, Affect and Aesthetic Moralism.* New York: Bloomsbury, 2017.

Thompson, Marie. "Whiteness and the Ontological Turn in Sound Studies." *Parallax* 23, no. 2 (2017): 266–82.

Tuck, Eve, and K. Wayne Yang. "Decolonization Is Not a Metaphor." *Decolonization: Indigeneity, Education and Society* 1, no. 1 (2012): 1–40.

Uexküll, Jakob von. *A Foray into the Worlds of Animals and Humans with a Theory of Meaning.* Translated by Joseph D. O'Neil. Minneapolis: University of Minnesota Press, 2010.

Umpleby, Stuart A. "Reviving the American Society for Cybernetics, 1980–1982." *Cybernetics and Human Knowing* 23, no. 1 (2016): 17–25.

Urban Dictionary. "Griefer." Accessed August 16, 2013. http://www.urban dictionary.com/define.php?term=griefer.

Walker, Bruce N., and Michael A. Nees. "Theory of Sonification." In *The Sonification Handbook*, edited by Thomas Hermann, Andy Hunt, and John G. Neuhoff, 9–40. Berlin: Logos, 2011.

Wallace, David Foster. *Everything and More: A Compact History of Infinity.* New York: W. W. Norton, 2003.

Williamson, Victoria. "Earworm Interview." *Music Psychology with Dr. Victoria Williamson* (blog), July 3, 2012. http://musicpsychology.co.uk/earworm-interview/.

Wolfe, Cary. *Ecological Poetics; or, Wallace Stevens's Birds.* Chicago: University of Chicago Press, 2020.

Wolfe, Cary. "Meaning as Event-Machine, or Systems Theory and 'The Reconstruction of Deconstruction.'" In *Emergence and Embodiment: New Essays on Second-Order Systems Theory*, edited by Mark B. N. Hansen and Bruce Clarke, 220–45. Durham, NC: Duke University Press, 2009.

Youngblood, Gene. *Expanded Cinema.* New York: Dutton, 1970.

INDEX

Page numbers in italics indicate key usages of a term.

abstraction and reality, 2
Adorno, Theodor, 1
aesthetic(s), 4, 90, 95, 99, 103
affect, 4
afterlife of data, 9, 106
algorithm, 12, 90–95, 128–29
analog, 76
art, art history, artworks, 7
(a)systematicities, 17, *106*
attention, 7–8, 56, 93, 106, 117. *See also*
　listening and hearing distinction.
　See also (in)attention.
attunement, 13, 17, 18, 60–61, 85, 95–99,
　102, 103, 115, 117, 118, 123
audition, post-computational, 106
aurality, 85

Bal, Mieke, 138n4
basketball, 117–23
Bateson, Gregory, 54, 70, 93, 112
beauty, 92
Beethoven, Ludwig van, 57
Behar, Katherine, 40
belief. *See* (dis)belief
Benjamin, Ruha, 137n30
Boetzkes, Amanda, 150n5
Bohr, Niels, 73

Brent, William, 15, 21, 128, 142n6,151n5,
　152n6
Brouwer, L. E. J., 69–70

Cage, John, 25–28, 92; whiteness and,
　139n16
cameras (in television and video
　games), 120, 122, 123
capitalism(s), 2, 7–11, 17, 40, 42, 103, 125.
　See also exchangeability, universal
causality, 57, 107, 114; computers and,
　65–67, 75, 80, 89; multicausal logics
　and, 17, 68, 106, 119; and reciprocal, 3;
　tautologies, 4
Chun, Wendy, 125
Church-Turing thesis, 81
Clark, Colin, *Freezing* (2015), 97–99, 103
climate change, 124
Clough, Patricia Ticineto, 3, 8–9
communication, 115, 127; collectives/
　teams and, 118–19; as a discipline,
　2–3; as impossible, 18, 129
computation, 71, 81, 115
computational data, 8, 36
computers, 36–37; human perception
　and, 63; linearity and, 65–68, 73;
　sound processing and, 76–77, 79, 81

conceptualism, 27, 139n18

"concert music," 23–24, 27, 57, 139n20

Connor, Steven, 8, 92, 114

Crawley, Ashon, 149n7

creative insight, 91

creative practice, 87, 89

Curry, Stephen, 120

data, 9–11, 18, 112, 137n40; acontextual atemporality and, 36; epidemiology and, 124–26; determinism and, 125; sound as, 37. *See also* afterlife of data

"datalities" of listening, 106. *See also* data; afterlife of data

dataphasia, 12, 40, 46, 68, 71, 74, 129, 137n41

Dean, Jodi, 12

Debussy, Claude, 100

decelerationism, 142n57

deconstruction, 28–31

Deleuze, Gilles, 4

Derrida, Jacques, 25, 130n37, 149n7. *See also* grammatology

Dewey, John, 8

disability studies, 137n40

(dis)belief, 9–10, 29, 72, 106, 125–26

(dis)embodiment, 45–46

Dittrich, Josh, 135

DNA (visualization), 85, 148n2

Doppler effect. *See* Fathead

dreams, 112–15

Duchamp, Marcel, 139n18

ear: physiology of the, 107–8, 110

Egan, Kelly, and *Ransom Notes* (2011), 86–89, 92, 98, 103

Eidsheim, Nina, 138n8

embodiment, 115, 117–19. *See also* (dis)embodiment

entrainment, 57, 96, 102–3, 119–20. *See also* learning

epidemiology, 124–26

Ernst, Wolfgang, 16, 66, 73–74

Evens, Aden, 37

excess, 4

exchange: datic, 9, 109, 129; logics of (morphology), 54

exchangeability, universal, 9, 10, 46, 65, 83, 106, 114; and scalability, 77. *See also* capitalism

excommunication, 5

exopistemological perspective, 8, 136n22

Exurbia (2011–14, with William Brent), 15–16, 21, *32–43*, 140n45, 140n46; and community, 40–42; and contingency, 39; downplayed visualization, 36; how it works, 33–35; temporality and, 37–39

Fathead, 16, *47–52*, 63–65, 82, 89, 95, 144n5; Doppler effects and, 49–50, 55; delay and, 51–53; its prehistory, 53–55

Fazi, M. Beatrice, 10–11, 16, 68, 71–74, 83, 110–11, 137n36, 137n38

Fourier (transform or integral), 16, 76–79

Fowler, Jarrod, *Kosuth to Fowler* (2006), 29–30

freesound.org, 90–93. *See also* Merz, Evan

Galison, Peter, 67

Galloway, Alexander, 8, 76

Galloway, Thacker, and Wark, 5

generality/universality and particularity, 1, 10–11, 18, 51, 65, 79, 81, 87–88, 98, 103, 110, 116–17, 151n1

GIF, 119–20

glitch art, 80, 147n59

Gödel, Kurt, 68–69, 136n33

Goldblatt, Robert, 69

grammatology, 23, 29–31, 108, 138n5

Greenberg, Clement, 23
griefing, 142n58
Gupta, Shilpa, *For, in Your Tongue, I Cannot Fit* (2017–18), 100, 103

Hagood, Mack, 82, 110, 148n64
Hall, Stuart, 8
hallucination, 8, 12, 65, 92, 108, 111–12; music as, 57
Hansen, Mark, 63, 73–75, 78
harmonic series, 146n50
Hartman, Saidiya, 136n28
Hayles, Katherine, 69; and the Regime of Computation, 91
hearing. *See* listening and hearing distinction
Heidegger, Martin, 118, 148n6
Hong, Sun-Ha, 9

Ikeda, Ryoji, *data-verse 1* (2019), 99–100, 103
(in)attention, 107
(in)coherence, 6, 18, 55–59, 63, 66, 89, 102, 103, 106, 112, 125, 135n10
incommunication, 5–8, 18, 40, 45, 47, 49, 51–52, 56, 60, 68, 74, 89, 93, 94, 97, 102, 106, 107, 109, 111, 112, 114, 118–19, 121, 123, 127, 129
incomputability, 72–73
infinitude, 71
innumerability, 71
intuitionist mathematics. *See* Brouwer, L. E. J.

JACK sound server, 129, 153n7
James, LeBron, 117–23
James, Robin, 13–14
James, William, 8, 94

Kahn, Douglas, 26, 142n3
Kim-Cohen, Seth, 21–25, 28–29, 93, 142n3
Kittler, Friedrich, 29

Kosuth, Joseph, *Text/Context* (1979), 29–30
Krauss, Rosalind, 23, 42
Kubisch, Christina, 93

Landauer's Principle, 146n47
Lastra, James, 45
Latour, Bruno, 136n23
Lear, Renée, *Renée Taking a Sip of Water (Human and Video in Motion)* (2013), 101–2, 103
learning, 95–96, 102
Leibniz and a "machine of thought," 10
listening, 13–14, 46, 85, *109–110*, 115, 149n23; active and resigned, 130; hearing distinction and, 106–8, 139n22; human-technology coupling and, 85; music and, 108; postcomputational, 106; scaling and, 112, 148n61; technicity and, 46, 89, 115
Lucier, Alvin, *I Am Sitting in a Room* (1969), 147n56

Madrigal, Alexis, 40
Malabou, Catherine, 141n47
Manning, Erin, 4–5, 44, 135n9
Marey, E. J., 99
material-semiotics, 13, 30, 84, *87*, 90, 101, 103, 127
Maturana, Humberto (et. al.), 54
Merz, Evan, and *Toll* (2012), 90–93
micro and macro distinctions, 74–75, 89
mistakes, misunderstandings, 53–54
Mitchell, W. J. T., 151n17
modeling, 125
Morris, Robert, 139n18
Moten, Fred, and Stefano Harney, 5
music, 24, 57, 108, 128, 138n5, 139n20, 141n54; musicians and, 24–25, 109; rhetoric of, 24–26, 42, 92, 139n9. *See also* listening; "concert music"

Index   165

Munster, Anna, 58–60, 92, 102–3, 121; and "generation of consistency," 60

Nancy, Jean-Luc, 84
neurodiversity. *See* Manning, Erin
Nintendo Entertainment System, 129
non-cochlear sound art. *See* Kim-Cohen, Seth

pandemic, 124–28, 130
Parisi, Luciana, 68
Pater, Walter, 23–24
pedestrian–mobile phone accident, 58–59
Peirce, Charles Sanders, 8
perspective, 55, 144n22
Peters, J. D., 2–4
Pivato, Julian, and *Yesterday Wants More* (2013–14), 95–97, 98, 103
Pollock, Jackson, 139n18
pragmatism, 14–15
Priest, Eldritch, 26
psychedelic adjacency, 112, 150n7

quantitative/qualitative shifts, 49, 121, 122. *See also* scaling
quantum mechanics, 136. *See also* Bohr, Niels

realism, 56
reciprocal causality. *See also* causality; Peters, J. D.
recording, 119
resonation, 114. *See also* Connor, Steven
Rilke, Rainer Maria, 28–29
Ringgold, Faith, 139n18
Roof, Judith, 149n7

scaling, 112, 119, 148n61. *See also* exchangeability; listening; whole and part
Scannell, R. Joshua, 9

Schaeffer, Pierre, 28
Schilling, Melissa, 91, 95
senses; and doubling, 45–46, 57; intersensory echo, 52; vertical stereophony, 53
Serres, Michel, 5, 12, 81, 135n13
Shannon, Claude, 36
sonic collective, 109. *See also* sound
sonic episteme, 13, 17
sonic pragmatism, 32, 35, 43
sonification, 93–94
sound, 24, 141n48; Cageanism and, 25–26; enabling conditions, 99, *110*, 115; fidelity and, 76–78; medium specificity and, 21, 23, 30, 32, 81; in opposition to visuality, 29–30; software spatialization, 36–38; synthesis, 76–78; its resistance to expression as data, 37–38
sound art, 27–30, 32, 43
sound studies, 135n13
Spivak, Gayatri Chakravorty, 138n5
Sprenger, Florian, 66–67
stapedius. *See* ear
stereo inversion, 44
Sterne, Jonathan, 31, 137n45, 148n62
squash, 116–17, 122–23
subjectivity, 126

technicity. *See* listening and technicity
television and televisuality, 118–19, 121
temporalities, 4, 17, 67, 75, 80, 102–3, 107; incommunication and, 111, 118. *See also* causality; time-criticality
Thacker, Eugene, 136n28
Thompson, Jessica, 45
Thompson, Marie, 6, 135n13
time-criticality, 16, 66, 73–79; and timbre, 147n52. *See also* computers: linearity
Tindale, Adam, 142n6

tinnitus, 82, 141n51, 148n64. *See also* Hagood, Mack

toothbrush, 111–12

Tuck, Eve, and K. Wayne Yang, 136n19

Tuning Speculation, 59, 144n27

Turing, Alan, 10, 69–71

Uexküll, Jakob von, 54

undo (command-Z), 113–14. *See also* causality; exchangeability; temporalities

video games, 120–23

Wallace, David Foster, 138n1

Whitehead, Alfred North, 5, 57, 111

whole and part, 6, *55*, 112. *See also* scaling

windowing, 79–80, 147n58

Youngblood, Gene, 23

zero, 22